Finding *Self*

Rediscover, reconnect and empower the *you* who has been forgotten

It's time to matter!

Brandy Douglas Corcoran

Finding Self

Although the author and publisher have made every effort to ensure that the information in this book was correct at press time, the author and publisher do not assume and hereby disclaim any liability to any party for any loss, damage, or disruption caused by errors or omissions, whether such errors or omissions result from negligence, accident, or any other cause.

Adherence to all applicable laws and regulations, including international, federal, state and local governing professional licensing, business practices, advertising, and all other aspects of doing business in the US, Canada or any other jurisdiction is the sole responsibility of the reader and consumer.

Neither the author nor the publisher assumes any responsibility or liability whatsoever on behalf of the consumer or reader of this material. Any perceived slight of any individual or organization is purely unintentional.

The resources in this book are provided for informational purposes only and should not be used to replace the specialized training and professional judgment of a health care or mental health care professional.

Neither the author nor the publisher can be held responsible for the use of the information provided within this book. Please always consult a trained professional before making any decision regarding treatment of yourself or others.

ISBN: 978-1-7779854-0-0

LET'S MAKE LIFE EVEN EASIER!

Reading this book is awesome but real change for *your life* happens when *you* do the work for yourself. The workbook portion within this book is designed for you to know *you* better and to create lasting breakthroughs.

I want to make that even easier with a handy workbook as my gift of thanks to you for getting my book.
Please download the Finding Self Workbook here:
brandyc.authorchannel.co

This workbook should be used alongside your book and it will help do the work to get back to *you*!
With inspirational quotes and workbook portions clearly laid out, you will have everything you need at your fingertips.

DON'T WAIT!

Say "YES" to creating a life you love:
Get started on your journey of self-discovery and find joy, fulfillment and how to love everything about your life today!
Girl, it's time to matter!

Dedication

This book is dedicated to my incredible parents who gave me life and continue to support, believe in and encourage me throughout every journey. Their example of unconditional love was the foundation for everything I dared to become. They are the source of my strength, courage and love. Raising such an exceptional woman was not an easy task and they did it with humour and dedication, being more committed to my own happiness than I was at times. I owe them my life; the beginning, middle and end! Job well done **Gary and Yvonne**!

To my beautiful daughters who are my reason for everything! **Emma and Isabella (Ella)**, you make me want to be the best version of myself because you both deserve nothing less. You are the reason that I know I am the daughter in whom God is well pleased as he trusted me to raise, and contribute to you two incredible souls! What a gift you have been to me and as I say in my book, I may have given you life but you have given it right back to me! "I love you more! Not possible!"

To my brave, loving and constantly supportive **tribe**. You show

me what makes life truly rich…relationships! You fill my soul, my cup and make my life beautiful! To name you all would take a whole other book but I pray and trust that I have not hidden my love and appreciation from you and you know this is for you! And within that tribe, I need to thank my incredible sister **Michelle**! You have ridden the storm with me more than you should have had to and I am beyond blessed to have such love and support. You are my rock!
And to my bestie **Sylvia**, you are the wind beneath my wings! Through your unconditional love, you taught me how to love myself and that has not always been an easy job. Not only did you save my life when we were younger, you continue to stand for it now and make me believe in myself!

And to my soulmate, my lover, my partner in adventure, laughter and love, **Travis T Libby**! I could not have done this without you solidly by my side. You so fiercely believe in me and accept nothing less than my own greatness which made it impossible for me to hide and play small. I fucking love us!

And **for moms** who feel like they have lost a sense of who they are and what brings them joy and fulfillment. I see you. I got you. I appreciate all you do and bring to the world! You are so much more than the stories you have told yourself!

"I love you. I'm sorry. Please forgive me. Thank you."
~Ho'oponopono prayer of reconciliation.

"And I said to my Self, 'I want to be your friend.'
My Self took a long breath and replied,
'I have been waiting my whole life for this.'

Foreward

When I helped co-found Norwex in 1998 in the small rural community of Dauphin, Manitoba, I knew that in the years ahead, I would meet some amazing people who wanted to help others succeed and change their world; Brandy Douglas Corcoran is one of those people. We first meet in 2006 at an event in Calgary, Alberta. She demonstrated her tenacity and focus right away, quickly building a successful business and a dedicated and growing team.

Brandy is real, authentic and passionate about life, personal growth and mentoring others to grow and find their authentic calling. Through the years we have travelled together on many trips and enjoyed beautiful destinations, having lots of fun in the process. We have also shared the ups and downs of life together as she pursued her own healing and helped many others through theirs.

In this book you will discover three things. How you can be free of the issues and pain that holds you back, celebrate the victories as you overcome and lastly discover your real and authentic self.

Embrace the journey ahead!

Debbie Bolton

Norwex Co-Founder

Content

CHAPTER ONE: Losing Self 11
CHAPTER TWO: Burying Self.. 19
CHAPTER THREE: Finding Self 27
CHAPTER FOUR: Loving Self.. 39
CHAPTER FIVE: HOPE - Hold On Pain Ends 47
CHAPTER SIX: The R-Word.. 57
CHAPTER SEVEN: None of it is Real 65
CHAPTER EIGHT: Journey Into Self.................................... 77
CHAPTER NINE: Weeds or Seeds 91
CHAPTER TEN: Moving Out.. 97
CHAPTER ELEVEN: Watch Your Mouth! 109
CHAPTER TWELVE: The Gift of Responsibility 117
CHAPTER THIRTEEN: False Evidence Appearing Real.... 129
CHAPTER FOURTEEN: Life's Purpose Fulfilled.............. 143
CHAPTER FIFTEEN: Bringing Your Dreams Alive 155
CHAPTER SIXTEEN: It Starts with Self 167
CHAPTER SEVENTEEN: Celebrate Everything!.............. 173

CHAPTER ONE

Losing Self

I forgot how exceptional I am. I do not mean special. I mean exceptional, with unique strengths, gifts, and ways of being and seeing the world. For a while there, life was piling on top of me, and I could not see clearly. I forgot that underneath the stories, the wounds, the heartbreak, and confusion, underneath the busy, the doubt, the fear, and the shame was an exceptional woman.

Somewhere along the journey, I had gotten lost. I had started to merely *survive* this experience called life. I lost my joy. I lost a sense of fulfillment. I lost myself.

I tried a million different ways to get love.

I was always trying to prove I was worthy. I was trying to prove my value by doing more and saying yes to all the things and all the people. I was trying to be someone others wanted to be around instead of focusing on being someone who I wanted to be around. I was busy and appeared happy and confident, while the whole time, I feared others would discover I was a fraud. The thoughts in my head screamed at me. "Imposter!" "Failure!" "You will never be good enough!" "Give up!" And all I could see in my life was evidence of how true those comments were.

I was exhausted.

The harder I tried, the more it felt like fulfillment and happiness eluded me. Sure, I had happy times and what appeared to be a great life. I adapted to that empty, unsettled feeling by being super grateful and positive. In fact, for all intents and purposes, it was a great life. So why was I not happy? Why was I not joyful, with the peace of mind to be truly free and thriving? Why was I not *that* kind of happy?!

I got into an endless cycle of thinking; if I just do X, then I will be happy.

Maybe this workout would be the key. Oh, I know; I will get up early and meditate to start my day. Perhaps if I read more? Maybe gluten is the problem? Maybe it is my kids? If they could just be more helpful and appreciative. Or is it my husband? He never really tells me that I am beautiful or that I am doing a good job. Why does no one see and appreciate all that I do?! Maybe the problem is not me but rather "out there?" Oh heck, I do not know? I bet this glass of wine will make me feel better! It will at least stop the thoughts for now.

It was an endless cycle of searching and shame, of two steps forward and one step back. I was exhausted and sad and barely hanging on most days. I could not figure out why my best was never good enough.

Then the bottom fell out!

My husband said, "You are what is wrong with my life. You are the reason I cannot be happy, and I am divorcing you." I felt like I had been hit by a tsunami. I was in an internal tornado of all the mistakes and regrets of my past. I was barely surviving the present and terrified of the unknown future. I did not know where I would be thrown or where I would finally land when the whirlwind stopped.

I hit rock bottom and could no longer run my "fake it till you make it" motto. I had to allow myself to call for help and let people see me in my mess. I stopped hiding behind an outward appearance of smiles and positivity. This started to let me see that I was not alone. I began feeling support and loving hands upon me, grounding me and trying to pull me out of the tornado that I was in.

But first, I had to pull for myself and make the choice to go on. I had to believe that life could get better and that there was a purpose to my pain.

"You must truly believe in the end of your own story. Where you are currently is not who you are unless you choose to stay there." ~ Tony Robbins

I remember the night my ex-husband left so clearly. It was a Saturday night, February 10th, 2018. He hugged the girls and me and left the "dream home" that we had built together, declaring that our marriage was done. He said, "You will be happier too."

I did not believe his words, but I clung to them for hope. The house felt so big and empty. My heart felt physically broken, as if shattered into a million little pieces. I had two beautiful humans who needed me, looking up at me for guidance, assurance, and strength. I remember hugging them and, through the tears, promising them we would be okay.

Truthfully, I was not sure we would.

In declaring to them that night that we would be okay, I heard it for myself. Those words, that declaration, the promise I made to my girls, planted a seed of possibility that has grown into this beautiful life I love. This blessed life that I did not see possible when I planted a little seed called, "we will be okay." It is as miraculous to me as the fact that a little acorn can grow into a sturdy oak tree.

I have so much compassion for myself when I look back on those days. I am in awe that I had the strength to get out of bed the next day, and the next day, and the day after that. It took so much strength and courage to make it through each day. I would count the hours until it was an acceptable time to crawl into bed at night so I could escape my pain and worry.

My strength and courage came from who I was committed to being for those girls. I had given them life, but during those turbulent times, they gave life back to me.

Then one day, my tears turned into gratitude!

Not for the whole day, but I experienced moments of gratitude throughout. Gratitude for this great cup of coffee. Gratitude for this hot shower. Gratitude for my home. Gratitude for my strength. A superhuman strength that I didn't even know I had. Gratitude for my growth. And gratitude for my tribe.

I started to trust that maybe God really doesn't give us more than we can handle. Something my mom used to say to build my strength and faith when I was younger.

And then I felt it.

I even had gratitude that my ex-husband had the strength to leave. That he knew we did not work anymore. Gratitude that he knew that the best parts of us could continue as great co-parents and friends, not as a married couple.

Today, I have gratitude for my new life and how it exceeds anything I could have imagined.

So why am I sharing this?

Because I am confident that if you are reading this book, you may be going through a tough time. Or you have made it through one.

I want to remind you that you have already overcome so much and that your darkest days *can* become your best life. I want to remind you that even when all hope feels lost, life always gets better. I want to be an example to you of what is possible, so you always hold on and keep going. Most of all, I want you to be happy, I want you to be great and I want you to share the gift of who you are with the world!

By picking up this book, you have already taken the first *right* step. You just need to take the next *right* step and then the next *right* step, and so on. Then one day, you will look back, and all those *right* steps will have led you to your best life. You will be so grateful that you kept taking them. You will see the strength and courage inside of you that you may not even know you have.

You are braver than you believe, stronger than you seem, and smarter than you know
~A.A. Milne

Before we begin our journey, let me address the part of you who has brought you this far in your life. *Thank you*! Thank you for a job well done to the best of your ability. I know you have brought many good things to many people, and I acknowledge you for that!

And now you are here because you want more. You want full self-expression, fulfillment, lasting joy, and purpose. You may need to give up some things and create new ways. Please give some space for this to happen. You do not need to fight for survival anymore.

You are *safe*.

You are *seen*.

You are *deeply appreciated* for getting us this far!

Let us begin this journey by starting to remember how *you* are truly exceptional.

What are your unique strengths, gifts, ways of being and seeing the world? Please do not be humble here. *Own that greatness* inside of you!

If you cannot own your greatness for yourself, then do it for others. Do it for the people around you who do not get the amazing gifts that you bring when you play small. Think about who loses when you do not allow yourself to win!

What is exceptional about me is:__________________________

____

____

____

Now be honest, how fun was it to spend some time acknowledging what is great about yourself? For some, it is a new experience from the self-deprecating way we can talk to ourselves. So often, we engage in conversations about what is wrong. It is much nicer to look at what is right! Remember, what is wrong is always available to see, but so is what is right!

Let us start today to build on all the exceptional things about you and your life!

Thank you for having the courage to join me on this exciting journey of *Finding Self*.

CHAPTER TWO

Burying Self

"Owning our story can be hard but not nearly as difficult as spending our lives running from it. Embracing our vulnerabilities is risky but not nearly as dangerous as giving up on love and belonging and joy - the experiences that make us the most vulnerable.
Only when we are brave enough to explore the darkness will we discover the infinite power of our light."

~Brene Brown

Like I said at the start of this book, I had forgotten how exceptional I was. It was not a conscious forgetting; it happened over time. Experience after experience, choice upon choice, until I woke up one day, looked around, and thought, "who am I, and how the hell did I get here?"

One way I see how I had forgotten is because shame loves secrecy. I was ashamed of pretty much everything, so I continued to hide and bury parts of myself. This had me feel more shame, which had me hide more and on and on it went. The shame spiral is a vicious process. And let me tell you, I worked hard to hide what I thought was so wrong about me.

Like a day at the beach getting buried in sand, things people said, experiences I went through, and my own thoughts piled on top of me until one day, all that was exposed of me was a false sense of happiness. To anyone who truly could see me, they knew. They saw the emptiness, the fear, the sadness, and the hopelessness. They could feel something was '*off*' about me. The forced smile and loud laugh were so incongruent with the sad eyes. I remember one wise woman told me that I was the most "unconfident, confident person" she knew. I am still shocked that she could see me. I thought I had fooled the world.

I used to have it as integral to my survival to be valuable and pleasing to people. I was not free to live life for myself or to be authentic in the moment if I thought it would go against what a person wanted me to be. It was a lot of work, and it hurt. I was intent on being a social chameleon. I thought it was the only way others would like me. One of the greatest human fears is to not be loved and to be abandoned. I would do anything to avoid that pain! I felt like I would lose a piece of my soul if everyone did not like me. Unbeknownst to me. I was losing a piece of my soul, trying to make everyone like me. I was exhausted. I was hurt. And I felt like I could never win.

And my goodness, the energy it took to keep up the forced positivity and perception of that false happiness! Existing felt like a lot of work. I tried my very best, worked as hard and fast as I could all day long, and still, it never felt good enough. *I* never felt good enough.

Shame was the context for my life. It was in everything, and it affected everything. I was trapped in it because, as far as I understood, I was it. *I was shame.*

When we are certain that something is wrong and we are no good, we cannot imagine sharing '*who we are*' with the world. We are certain that if people '*see us,*' they will judge us and take away their love. As a child, that feels like certain death. We rely on love and care from a young age so it is no surprise that it feels we may not survive losing love and being abandoned as adults. All that reinforces the story in the shame cycle and feeling like we need to hide parts of ourselves.

I would keep people at arm's length in fear of being discovered as a fraud. It was so tough because I truly love people and got joy being with them. But shame told me I needed to keep my distance, stay safe, and keep hiding my '*not good enoughness.*' I was certain that if others knew my truth that '*something was wrong*' with me, they would take away their love and acceptance. Is there something you think is wrong or bad about you? Do you spend energy trying to hide something that you feel shame about? Do you remember a moment when you decided that something was wrong with you or in the wold?____________________

____

____

____

I took on stories I had been told from my well-meaning parents, teachers, and some mean kids as the truth about me. Once we identify with a story and believe it, we are stuck! It becomes another layer of what buries our sense of self. It guides our thoughts and actions about what we are capable of and what we deserve. This is because the strongest need we have as human being is for consistency in our identity—to be '*true*' to ourselves.

The problem begins when that 't*rue self*' limits us or is just a plain old lie.

If you think about it, we do not live in our lives and relationships. We live in the stories we tell ourselves about them, which are largely given to us as we grow up. We are told a story about who we are, but thankfully it is just a story.

What are you certain that you know about yourself? Who do you say you are? It may start with when you say things like, "Oh, I'm not X. Or I would never. Or I always Y" It may appear to be negative or positive. Try not to judge it. This exercise is for you to see how you perceive yourself and what stories you are telling. It is an opportunity for you to begin to see your self-image and what you are working so hard to maintain. You may begin to see why you feel stuck when you try to make lasting changes.

Start with how you would describe yourself, and then what you are certain you are not. Write freely. There are no right or wrong answers. ______________________________

____

If you have not written anything, stop reading and go jot down at least a few '*truths*' before you read on. I am about to tell you the dangerous thing about identity and the things '*good*' or '*bad*' that you wrote.

Our thoughts become our reality. Read that again! Our thoughts *become our reality*.

It is not that we think something because it is the truth. It is the truth because we think it.

I know you may have years and years and example after example of how '*true*' something is and how '*right*' you are about that thing. But remember, our *thoughts* become our *reality*.

Let us consider another way of looking at it. Consider that you see it *because* you believe it. Do you like being told you are wrong? Most people answer no to that. So when you believe something, you seek evidence for it so you can confirm how smart and right you are. You literally look for *your truth* in the world. And if you do not see it, your mind will make experiences fit your beliefs.

Where does that need for knowing and creating an identity for ourselves and others come from? Does being certain about something make you feel safe in the world? Would it make a difference in how you approach life and relationships if you did not feel like you knew what to expect? If we could not predict what was going to happen or how someone would treat us, what would your level of anxiety be?

Knowing is one of the six basic human needs. You need certainty. You need to understand the world so that you can predict it and ensure your safety and survival.

Here is the thing, if you are reading this book, you want more than merely surviving life. I am guessing that you are looking for ways to not just survive but to truly thrive. To stand powerfully as the person your soul calls you to be! To make the difference you were created to make and to know that because you lived, people's lives were made better. I am guessing that at the end of your life, you want to have used up everything you have been given and to have played your *best* game of life!

Like a house that our bodies live in, we live in an emotional home that we consistently return to. An emotional state we are used to and that we find comfort in, especially during challenging experiences. It is an automatic response, much like the fight or flight response. Our emotions are a habit we have developed and strengthened with our consistent behaviour. This is a key area to master so as to be able to create anything in your life and not be taken out when upset.

Would you not love to be able to turn moments of upset into something more positive and helpful? Throughout this book, we will build you a new emotional home that empowers you and leads you forward. We are going to do it by focusing on what you want. We are going to build the new instead of fighting the old. We are letting go of blaming ourselves, blaming others and playing the shame game.

This journey of discovery and healing will be taken with lightness, joy and courage.

Let us release and *unbecome* everything that no longer serves us and powerfully reconnect to the parts of ourselves that we have abandoned and buried.

Let us welcome ourselves home into our own strong and loving arms!

How much would you love to know what it feels like to show up for yourself?! To trust your word, to have the experience of having your own back? How much would you love to develop a healthy, positive, and loving relationship with the person in the mirror?

Honouring yourself is an *absolute must*!

I am personally inviting you on this incredible journey of self-discovery and fulfillment with me. I know you may feel anxious and scared to face the unknown. I know it can feel hard to grow and to transform but know this is normal. Know you are not alone.

I got you!

More importantly, by opening these pages and showing up here, *you got you*! And that is what matters!

It can also be helpful and enjoyable if you find a like-minded friend or family member to get a copy of this book to go through the journey together. Or you may choose someone safe to share your discoveries with as you go through it. As scary as that may seem, by sharing what you discover about yourself with a safe person, you will ground your discoveries and bring them to life. You and what you want for your life, as a new possibility, will exist in the world outside of yourself.

I am also inviting; no, I am *insisting* that you play full out here! You are playing for your life!

Read some of this book every day and do the work inside these pages. Engage in your life and transformation. This book is not for you to read to get to know me better or to gain some more knowledge. It is for you to get to know *you* better and for *you* to make a positive and lasting difference in *your life*!

You are worth whatever amount of time you need!

Let me say that again.

You are worth whatever amount of time you need!

It is never too late! The lost girl that you may have abandoned, neglected, mistreated or abused is still there within you and is waiting for you to return home to yourself.

Let's begin.

"Maybe the journey isn't so much about becoming anything. Maybe it's about unbecoming everything that isn't really you, so you can be who you were meant to be in the first place."

CHAPTER THREE

Finding Self

"All that we are is the result of what we have thought. The mind is everything. What we think, we become." ~Buddha

For most of my life, I was certain I did not matter and the world was a confusing place. I do not mean I had a *thought* about this; I mean I was *certain*! Like, I knew this to be a truth deep down in my soul. It was the very eyes with which I saw myself, all of life and every relationship.

The challenging part about this was that I was not aware it was *just a thought*.

I lived like it was the truth to the point that I could not even see the thought as separate from me. I imagine it would be like trying to explain to a fish what water is and that there is more that exists outside of the water. To the fish, the water is their existence. It is the reality that they swim in. Just as the *thought*,

"I do not matter," was the reality I swam in. There was no separation between my *thought* and my *identity*.

Freedom can be found in knowing that you *have thoughts,* but you are *not your thoughts*. This can be easier said than done, especially if you are not even aware of them!

That is why transformation and growth begin with awareness.

Once I identified this *thought* of "I do not matter," I could see it when it showed up. This made me aware that my *thought* was separate from me. I could choose a different one that worked *for me* versus *against* me. It was that simple.

I said simple. Not always easy.

Where did I get the ability to see a thought that had run my life for forty-one years as not the truth? Where did the desire to want to change that belief come from after all those years?

As we all know, change can be challenging and confronting, so why bother?

The *ability* to change my thoughts came from asking the right questions about my life. Then, my willingness and commitment to look and be honest with myself gave me the ability to go deeper.

The *desire* came when I saw the impact on my life as a result of believing that I did not matter and that the world was confusing.

Here is what that life looked like for me.

If I was not invited to an event, it was extremely upsetting because I *knew* that not getting invited was because I did not matter. This confused me because I knew people liked me, and

I had done my very best at being so kind and fun so as to ensure others would want to include me. I would feel so hurt, rejected and confused.

If my ex-husband did not want to be intimate with me, I would cry myself to sleep because, *of course*, it was about me not being good enough. How could I expect that he would want someone who did not matter? But I did not understand what was wrong because I knew he loved me. Again, more proof of how the world was such a confusing place!

I obsessively thought about what was wrong and spent so much energy trying to make sense of the confusing world. I made meaning *everywhere*. If my children did not clean up, it was not just a mess. I would blow up because the mess *was proof* that I did not matter. If I mattered, they would clean up! If I did not get the success I wanted from my team at work, it was because I had no influence because I did not matter. And I was confused about why my influence did not matter because I really was trying to be helpful. I could not lose weight and get real results with my health goals because I did not matter. Truthfully, I did not take the time and effort for myself because I unconsciously believed I did not deserve the time and effort. Why? Because I did not matter! And on and on it went!! If you feel exhausted reading this, imagine living it.

Remember, I did not know at the time that all this was occurring to me because of the *thought* that I did not matter. It was just what life was like for me.

And how did I feel?

I was exhausted! I was sad! I was overwhelmed! I felt hopeless!

Until I became a mom, suicide was always an option. Because really, did it matter if I was even here? I did not matter, so how could my being here matter? I was so tired of living in a world that hurt and confused me.

Every day I would dig in with grit and positivity only to be going to bed most nights feeling like I failed *once again* to move the needle forward in my life. It was never, ever good enough!

I was never, ever good enough!

I could not see the good I achieved. I would downplay all the success I accomplished because how could anything I was doing matter if I did not?

The end of one goal would always be the beginning of the next because I was so desperate to prove that I mattered and that I deserved to be here. There was no end in sight.

I am sharing my journey because I know we are similar. In describing the impact of these limiting beliefs on my life, I hope you can see what may be holding you back. By sharing my ability to transform them, I want you to realize that you can change your life too. My wish is for you to see that you are not alone in the way you suffer. I am on this journey with you.

Look at what you wrote in the previous chapter about what you are *certain* about yourself. How do you see these certainties influence your life? In what ways do the beliefs show up in your physical reality? Where do you see your beliefs in your life? Take a few minutes, it probably will not be obvious right away.

____

____

____

____

What has believing these things cost you? Look at jobs, relationships, joy, a sense of fulfillment, celebration or love. ___

____

____

____

____

Here is the thing about certainties or beliefs. Even the *good* ones limit you in some way because it stops you from anything outside of *that* belief. If I am certain I am kind, which is something I think is "good' to be, what happens when a situation occurs where I need to stop being kind? Consider that maybe then it would not be possible for me to *not* be kind because, well, I am *certain* that I am. If I identify as a kind person, any other behaviour that I do not view as that would not be me. Therefore, *not being kind* is outside my scope of possibility. Positive or negative beliefs about oneself are a limitation to your self-expression and freedom.

Sometimes, dangerously so.

The most impactful example in my life of where I suffered as a result of my need to not hurt someone's feelings happened when I was sixteen. I was dating an older guy, and we were hanging out in his room. He went to have a shower and told me to be naked by the time he came back. I was not comfortable with that, and everything in my mind and body screamed, "get out!" I went to leave, but his roommates were in the living room. I did not want to look stupid or hurt his feelings by over reacting, so I went back up, telling myself, *you will be fine*. I was not fine. When he was done taking what he wanted, he told me, "The next guy you are with will thank me." He had taught me that my body was not mine but that it was to be *used by* someone *else*. It was as if my cries of "stop" and "no" were not really happening. My voice had no power. I had no power. I felt like a thing, not a person. The situation reinforced my belief that I had no value and did not matter. I attempted to take my life shortly after that incident. Thankfully, my best friends and parents supported me through that attempt and got me counselling.

The important lesson for me to take from this experience was that because I identified as kind and valued not upsetting others, I forfeited my safety. Being kind had me ignore that voice inside of me that knew what was best for me. I was also carrying with me the limiting belief that I did not matter. Put these two beliefs together, kindness and not worthy, and we have a disaster zone. I will say it again, beliefs about oneself, whether they are positive or negative, are a limitation to your self-expression and freedom.

What is an identity you have that limits or hurts you? ______

____

Want to know the secret of how to create what you want for yourself and your life? You become what you believe. Let me say that again.

You become what you believe.

How exciting is that to hear? Are you starting to see the kind of power that you have to create your life and how you experience it? Is it becoming clear to you that you are the product of your thoughts? Are you starting to see some possibility for change and having what you want?

Maybe it is not that you need years of therapy, a new marriage, a job or another diet. Maybe, just maybe, it is just that you need to change your beliefs about your identity? Could it be that easy? Could the world really be your oyster?

Yes, it can!

Your beliefs are the lenses through which you exist in the world and through which the world exists for you. Your language reflects what those beliefs are. It is especially important to understand that whatever follows the words after '*I am*' will come looking for you. So be aware of what you say with your words and in how you speak in your mind with the thoughts you have.

To get what you want, you need to ask yourself, what do I believe? What thoughts follow '*I am?*' Look at how you are certain that identity includes the roles you do. When I ask you who you are, you may say things like; I am a mother. I am a wife. I am a doctor. For the most part, those things are not who you are; they are roles. That is an important distinction because when you do not see that it is a role versus who you are, it defines you and limits you. Not that the role is bad but if it defines you, then what happens when that role changes or is taken away? You might find yourself in an existential crisis. You might not know who you are without being a wife, mother, or doctor.

Let us look at your '*I ams.*' Do not judge the thought. Just fill in the blanks.

I am ____________. I am ____________. I am ____________

I am ____________. I am ____________. I am ____________

I am ____________. I am ____________. I am ____________

I want to address that part of you that is certain that what you know about yourself is true. The part of your mind that would give me example after example of stories and proof of why what you believe is actually true. I get it. It is hard not to believe something that you *think you saw*. The tricky part is that beliefs are formed by what we *think we see,* not necessarily what is so. Plus, remember that you see it because you believe it, which reinforces the belief. No amount of evidence to the contrary can get rid of strongly held beliefs.

I always felt like a chubby loser, not smart enough, and a failure as a kid growing up. I would look at my pretty, athletic, popular older sister and see all the things she was as evidence of what I was not. I believed there was only a finite amount of goodness, and if she possessed a characteristic or trait, it was not available to me.

However, years later, when I was in my late thirties, I was visiting my parents, and my mom showed me a scrapbook she had made from my childhood memories. There were articles upon articles of what a great athlete I was, ribbons and awards for my academics and other achievements. I was stunned! I remember saying to her; maybe I was not the loser I thought I was. Even now, I still hear from others that I am hard on myself. When a belief like '*not good enough*' exists, it is really hard to see any evidence to the contrary. We either dismiss it, or literally, we do not even see it. And even when we become aware of a limiting belief, we can still slip back into it as it is that old comfortable, familiar emotional house we once lived in.

Let me tell you this; I am not here to tell you what is true or not true about you. I do not know your life or your experiences. This book is about the energetic truth that our thoughts create our reality. Our beliefs are the invisible force that controls everything. Think of your beliefs as your success blueprint. You and your life become what you think. I have even heard it said that the happiness of your life depends upon the quality of your thoughts.

Want more happiness, have better thoughts!

Transformation and letting go are not about being right or wrong, bad or good. It is the willingness to look honestly at yourself and your life. It is getting clear on your thoughts about yourself, others, and the world. And it is about looking at what is dialogging in the space between your ears? What are the beliefs that are creating your life as you know it? What are you seeing *because* you believe it to be so?

Just start to consider that maybe what you are so certain of is not the truth. You have to be willing to let go of certainty and knowing.

Look at your current life. Where do you see your beliefs show up? Is there an area in your life that you are not satisfied with? What thoughts do you see there? What do you see as a pattern of thought that consistently shows up in your life?__________

____

____

____

In moments of upset or frustration, what are you telling yourself about what is happening and what it means about you? What are you telling yourself it means about the other person? What about the world? You may identify these beliefs by completing these sentences:

Again, there are no right or wrong answers. See what shows up for you.

I am ____

____

People are____________________________________

____

The world is____

____

I am not here to take anything away. You can have your limiting beliefs as long as you want to defend them. Did you hear me? You can keep those limiting beliefs if you want to.

I am just asking you to look at where those beliefs are reflected in your life and the impact they have. Then ask the hard truth about whether that serves you and whether that is making you happy.

We are driven in life to either seek pleasure or avoid pain. Avoiding pain is often the bigger motivator. Allow yourself to experience the impact; the loss, the pain and suffering, the unfulfilled love and missed opportunities that have resulted from your limiting beliefs and trust me, the *desire to* change will be there!

Remember, you can be right, or you can have results. Would you rather be right or have the results you say you want?

It may seem automatic to say, "Well, of course, I want the results I want!" Part of our human condition, however, is an almost aggressive need to be right. We are hardwired that knowing brings safety. We needed to know what the signs were if that sabre tooth tiger was coming for us and what to do about it quickly! That is why we fight to prove our rightness even against what we say we want and sadly, sometimes against who we say we love. Let me be the first to tell you.— there are no more sabre tooth tigers coming for you. It is safe for you not to know.

So in this more conscious state, I ask again:
Do you want to be right, or do you want results?
Do you want to be right, or do you want to be loving?
Do you want to be right, or do you want to be happy?

CHAPTER FOUR

Loving Self

Butterflies cannot see how beautiful their wings are. People are like that too.

Sometimes you can see fundamental limiting beliefs running your life if you go back as far as possible to when you first had the experience of a loss of power, freedom, self-expression or peace of mind.

For me, it was when I was six years old. There was a twelve-year-old boy who I looked up to and had a little kid crush on. He molested me for a period of a few weeks by getting me to touch him on top of his clothes, and he would touch me over mine.

This experience profoundly impacted my sense of self and my sense of the world. This was when I started to believe, "I do not matter." and "the world is confusing." Outside of this '*secret special*' time when he gave me attention, he was so mean to me otherwise. He would tease and pick on me in front of others but then would lay beside me and touch me and have me touch him in a way that felt special. In my six-year-old brain, the way I made sense of this was, "I must not matter." Sexual attention was confusing, and then being rejected after his attention confused me further. Many of my other limiting beliefs and ways of surviving in the '*confusing*' world were formed from this experience.

Sexual abuse and molestation are big experiences to make sense of in the mind of a child and are challenging to unravel as an adult.

Now I know that story may be upsetting to read, but it is part of my story. I asked you to show up to this journey with courage, so I need to as well. Trust me, it is hard, but it is also liberating. Remember, shame loves secrecy. To stop the shame I felt about this, I had to stop keeping the secret.

Everybody's experience of loss of power, freedom, peace of mind or self-expression is unique. We do not measure our experience against anyone else's. The significance is the thoughts you created about yourself and about the world in these moments, combined with the decisions you made about yourself, others and life in general. These thoughts and decisions end up running you subconsciously and creating what you see as reality.

What is a moment that jumps out to you as significant? Try not to judge it; just look. It might not even make sense at first. I thought mine was silly, and I had shame about it. I was confused and questioned whether I should have been more traumatized by the molestation over the lack of attention outside of it?! But attention feels good; ridicule does not. I no longer judge my sweet young self, who made sense of the world in the best way I could at that age and experience.

I also do not judge my sweet older self, who makes sense of the world in the best way I can at this age and experience.

We are always doing our best!

To help you see a significant moment in your life, ask yourself, what happened to you that had you create these beliefs about yourself and your world? Remember, you are safe now. You are just looking back. You are not actually back there. __________

____

____

____

What thoughts did you form in this moment? What did you decide this experience meant about you, other people and the world in general?____

____

____

____

The thing to remember is that the thought that was created was not a conscious choice. Not at all!

My thought of '*I do not matter*' was there in an attempt to explain this challenging experience. I had a limited understanding of myself and the world. I had a six-year-olds understanding. No wonder it felt like I was so stuck and powerless to make real change or to experience lasting joy and fulfillment as a grown woman. I was still being run by the thoughts a six-year-old had made up.

The amazing thing about seeing and resolving limiting beliefs is that all of a sudden, the impossible becomes possible. We see ourselves, the world and people in a new light. Even our relationships alter.

Can you imagine being in a relationship or interaction with someone who is sure they do not matter, and that life is a confusing place? Simply put, you cannot win. You cannot have a healthy relationship. You cannot contribute to them, and it is hard to understand why they are not hearing what you are saying. You are left with your love not having any place to land, which is upsetting and sad.

People loved me and kept trying, but they were often left with a sense of frustration and not being able to help me. Their love could not be let in as it did not fit with my thought paradigm of '*I do not matter.*' And remember, we do not like to be wrong. You will only see in the world the things that fit what you believe.

You see it because you believe it.

If something or someone did express that I mattered, I would downplay or dismiss it or focus on the one negative thing instead. How could I ever really celebrate my successes? Unbeknownst to me at the time, the filter '*I do not matter*' skewed the colour of *everything*! I would either figure people were just being nice or lying. I thought that my success was luck. Sometimes, I literally would not even hear the kind acknowledging words someone said and would actually hear it negatively. Bananas right?!

Look at your life; where do you see you are hard on yourself? Do you ever acknowledge, thank or celebrate *yourself*? Do you appreciate the many little ways you show up, or does it have to be huge before you acknowledge or celebrate yourself? How often do you fall into comparing yourself to others and feeling less than? Sadly, it is so easy!______________________________

____

____

____

My life changed when I stepped outside of the horrific stories of what I had been through and saw the hard truth about those stories. It changed when I began to understand what had done the real damage. Or should I say '*who?*'

What I saw was that out of all the ways people had abused, abandoned, mistreated and neglected me, what hurt me the most was the ways in which I had done that to myself! Because no matter what happens in life, if I did not have my own back, I felt truly alone and like life was hopeless.

How do you feel when you look at ways that you have abused, abandoned, mistreated and neglected self?____________________

____

____

____

Let that sink in for yourself. You have done nothing wrong. There is nothing to deny or defend. You did what you did, and you did not do what you did not do. I truly believe that we are always doing the best we can based on where we are at mentally, emotionally, physically and spiritually.

Awareness is the first step. Just be willing to look at your life honestly.

Look at the times in your life where you have abused, abandoned, mistreated and neglected yourself and how that has created the struggles that show up in your life today.

What are some of the ways and times that you see you have not had your own back?________________________

____

____

____

What do you see is the impact of the times you have not had your own back? How has it effected you and the results in your life?______________________________________

____

____

____

One of the first steps I took to develop a loving relationship with myself was to start a Self-Appreciation Journal. Like a Gratitude Journal, I would write down three things I appreciated about myself every day. It felt weird and was difficult when I started. I would think and think and then start with things like,

Well, I am having a good hair day, or *I got out of bed.* Honestly, it was that simple, and that is okay! Start where you are. Keeping a Self-Appreciation Journal takes a willingness. You have to be willing to release how certain you are that you are no good and that something is wrong with you.

You have to be willing to feel better about yourself.

What are at least three things that you appreciate about *you* today?____

____

____

____

I understand that looking inward for answers and what is there can be exhausting and heavy. I acknowledge you for showing up and looking. Remember, we are always doing the best we can with where we are at and what we are aware of.

The exciting news is that you can start *today*, right here, right now, *to thrive*!

You can create a life that honours and excites you. A life you truly love!

"It is vital that you see yourself and accept yourself as a goddess. You can work out endlessly, starve yourself skinny, stuff yourself fat, envy the glamorous celebrities, but none of these pursuits will satisfy you on their own accord. The key to happiness lies within your capacity for self-love. And the key to self-love, in turn, lies within your willingness to embrace your authentic Self, your inner goddess."

For those of you who do not see how brave and amazing you are for picking up a book like this and doing the work to pull out your best self, let me be the first to say I see you, and you *are fucking phenomenal*!!!

I invite you to be the second to say it to yourself. Put this book down and go look in the mirror, stare right into your eyes and say, "I am phenomenal! I am fucking phenomenal!" Try to say it and mean it. "I am phenomenal!" And if you cannot go to "phenomenal", start with "I am pretty great!" Or "I am doing my best today!"

You really are a true gift! As Mel Robbins says, go high-five that phenomenal woman in the mirror. Tell her you love her. Tell her that you are showing up for her!

CHAPTER FIVE

HOPE - Hold On Pain Ends

"Just when the caterpillar thought its life was over, it became a butterfly."

I spent a lot of my teenage and young adult years wanting to die. I do not know if I really wanted to die; I just did not want to live. At least not in the experience of life that I was having. It felt too hard. Too grey. Too hopeless. The emotional pain was so strong and real that it felt physical. Maybe instead of wanting to die, I just wanted the pain to stop. Do you ever feel like you are at the end of your rope? You know you will not let go but at the same time, holding on feels like so much work? Every. Single. Day.

I wish someone had told me then that I was creating my own reality. I probably would not have believed it, but it would have given me a sense of hope that maybe I was not just cursed to have a hard life. I would have started to think that maybe things would get better.

I also wish someone had told me that these worst days would turn into my best life and that everything I was going through had a purpose. I wish I could see that the challenges were developing my strength, empathy, wisdom and courage. I wish I knew that this broken version of me would become the best version of me. What if I had thought about the fact that even for a star to be born, a gaseous nebula must collapse? That it was okay to collapse, to crumble and to break down all the things that did not serve my true self being able to shine.

I wish someone had told me the words from one of my favourite Trent Shelton youtube videos that I watched on repeat through the early days of my divorce.

> **Sometimes it takes certain things falling apart for better things to fall in place. Sometimes it takes losing what you're settling for to remind you of what you truly deserve. Sometimes it takes the most uncomfortable paths to lead your life to the most beautiful place.**
>
> **You will never see the purpose of the storm until you see the growth it produced. You will never see the purpose of someone leaving your life until you see what's best for your life. You will never understand why you're going through what you're going through until you see the strength, the power, the growth that it built inside of you.**
>
> **Your current situation is not your final destination. This storm will eventually run out of rain. This struggle that seems like it's lasting forever will eventually run out of pain. This hurt you, will turn into the greatest you. This broken you, will turn into the best you.**

Let these hard times turn into your best times. Let these bad days create your best days. Like the proverb says, just when the caterpillar thought its life was over, it became a butterfly.

Just because something is over, doesn't mean your life is over. This chapter is not your story. This moment is not your identity. This pain is not your life.

This pain will become power. This weakness will become strength. This confusion will become peace. Better things are coming for your life. Everything you're going through, will eventually turn to everything you made it through.

Your heart will heal. your tears will dry. Your mind will calm. Every single day is a new beginning...make today yours! It all starts with you! Trent Shelton

What if you knew that everything was going to work out in the end? Would that help you show up in your life in a new way?

One of the best acronyms I read was: HOPE - Hold On Pain Ends.

I did not know how the pain would end when I was in the middle of it, but even just hearing the word 'hope,' and that translation gave me the strength to continue hanging on. You must believe in the end of your story. Where you are is not *who* you are!

Have you ever heard the phrase that life is happening *for* you and not *to* you? It is the idea that everything that feels hard right now is stretching, growing and developing you for something more. That even though we may not see it at the moment, what feels heavy and hard is in service to your best life. Everything that you have experienced in your life gives you the strength to separate from what no longer serves you?

I think this is beautifully expressed in the story of the caterpillar's struggle to become a butterfly.

A man found a cocoon. One day a small opening appeared. He sat and watched the butterfly for several hours as it struggled to force its body through that little hole. Then it suddenly stopped making any progress and looked like it was stuck. So the man decided to help the butterfly. He took a pair of scissors and snipped off the remaining bit of the cocoon. The butterfly emerged easily, although it had a swollen body and small, shrivelled wings.

The man did not think anything of it and sat there waiting for the wings to enlarge to support the butterfly. But that did not happen. The butterfly spent the rest of its life unable to fly, crawling around with tiny wings and a swollen body. Despite the man's kind heart, he did not understand that the restricting cocoon and the butterfly's struggle to get itself through the small opening were the universe's way of forcing fluid from the butterfly's body into its wings. The struggle was needed to prepare the butterfly for flying.

Our struggles develop our strengths.

Sometimes the universe gives us exactly what we *need* to progress to the next chapter in our story, even if it is not what we *want*. The surprising truth about enough and sufficiency is the exquisite experience of being met by the universe with exactly what you need, exactly when you need it. It may come in the form of a divorce, a cancer diagnosis, the death of a loved one, losing a job, or an unhappy marriage. There are many hard things we endure in life. However, consider there is a plan to these struggles, and just as the butterfly struggled, it is happening *for* you.

You are made to do hard things!

I look back now at the many threads of how things happened *for me* and how they set me up to be at this perfect place in life right now, and it all makes sense. I am so grateful that I did not give up and that I kept taking the next *right* step.

Stop, look and listen. Your life is speaking to you. Are you paying attention to what it is saying?

"Every experience, no matter how bad it seems, holds within it a blessing of some kind.

The goal is to find it." ~Buddha

What feels like a tough spot or situation will launch your best life when you persevere, learn the lessons from the struggle and apply the '*right*' formula.

What are some tough times that you have been through? Maybe it is mistakes you have made or things that have happened *to* you. List all the tough stuff here. Be free. This is just for you.

____

____

____

____

Look at the list above. What positive things came from these experiences? A new relationship, a new quality that you developed, a new way of being, an opportunity to show yourself your strength, a new career, time off with the people you love, time to reflect and slow down, or a chance to pivot? Allow yourself to see the blessings that came out of the list above and write them down.____

____

____

____

"If you want to find happiness, find gratitude."

Awesome job! You know it takes real strength of heart and willingness to look at the blessings and step into a space of gratitude, especially for the challenging experiences.

Remember to say, "thank you." Thank you to yourself for getting through the challenges and learning your lessons. And thank you to the universe/God for providing the tough stuff so you could grow and develop. And I mean *really* be thankful!

Stop reading—hand on your heart. Eyes closed. Get present to that time and the lesson that came from it. Let your whole heart fill with gratitude for that scared, strong being who carried you through it. That is *you* I am talking about!

Do you know what is cool? That experience of true gratitude is within you any time you choose to stop and experience it!

"Tough times don't last. Tough people do."

I know looking inward and growing can be hard work, but so is staying stuck and feeling powerless. Letting go of long standing beliefs and your proof about all you know to be true can be hard, but so is staying angry and missing new opportunities. Transforming your beliefs takes repetition and commitment, which can seem hard. But you know what is harder?

Letting the pain of your past dictate the pain in your present.

Choose your hard!

Ask yourself, do you want to be right or happy? Do you want to be right or do you want to have the results that your heart is pulling you towards? The choice is yours!

As you do the work, have HOPE. Hold On Pain Ends. All the tough stuff you are going through will eventually be the tough stuff that you made it through. One thing you can guarantee is that everything changes. Nothing will stay the same forever.

And remember, you are so much more than the bad things that have happened to you.

In fact, maybe those "bad things" happened *for you.*

Me: Hey God.

God: Hello.....

Me: I'm falling apart. Can you put me back together?

God: I would rather not.

Me: Why?

God: Because you aren't a puzzle.

Me: What about all of the pieces of my life that are falling down onto the ground?

God: Let them stay there for a while. They fell off for a reason. Take some time and decide if you need any of those pieces back.

Me: You don't understand! I'm breaking down!

God: No - you don't understand. You are breaking through. What you are feeling are just growing pains. You are shedding the things and the people in your life that are holding you back. You aren't falling apart. You are falling into place. Relax. Take some deep breaths and allow those things you don't need anymore to fall off of you. Quit holding onto the pieces that don't fit you anymore. Let them fall off. Let them go.

Me: Once I start doing that, what will be left of me?

God: Only the very best pieces of you.

Me: I'm scared of changing.

God: I keep telling you - YOU AREN'T CHANGING!! YOU ARE BECOMING!

Me: Becoming who?

God: Becoming who I created you to be! A person of light and love and charity and hope and courage and joy and mercy and grace and compassion. I made you for more than the shallow pieces you have decided to adorn yourself with that you cling to with such greed and fear. Let those things fall off of you. I love you! Don't change! ... Become! Become! Become who I made you to be. I'm going to keep telling you this until you remember it.

Me: There goes another piece.

God: Yep. Let it be.

Me: So ... I'm not broken?

God: Of course Not! - but you are breaking like the dawn. It's a new day. Become!!!

~Author John Roedel

CHAPTER SIX

The R-Word

"The moment you accept responsibility for everything in your life is the moment you gain the power to change anything in your life."

So how do you turn the tough stuff into the best stuff?

You need the R-Word. Responsibility!

First, let me say you are not stuck! You are simply committed to patterns of thinking and behaviour because they are what has gotten you through in the past. You are not stuck or broken. You have a pattern, a habitual way of thinking and acting that keeps producing the same results. Those thoughts and behaviours have become more harmful and limiting rather than helpful in moving you forward at this point in your life. And they are based on survival. But you are not here to survive, you are here to thrive!

Again, the reason why you have not moved forward is not that you are broken or not good enough or need to be fixed. It is because you keep applying old thoughts and behaviours to get to a new level in your life. Change the formula, and you will change your life.

But how do you change the formula? How do you take thoughts and behaviours that have been embedded for years into your way of being and create something new? It starts with taking the responsibility to see that life is not happening *to* you. It is *responding to you*. You are not a victim in your life. You are actually the captain of the ship.

Begin by seeing that you are where you are because *you have outdated beliefs about yourself and life.* Those beliefs create feelings, and then you act on those feelings which gets you the results that you have. So as much as we all have a list of people and things that are responsible for our lives, it all begins with us and our beliefs. Point to something with just your index finger and repeat after me, "You are responsible for this." What you might notice is that although we try to blame the thing outside of ourselves, you have three fingers pointing back at you!

The power for your life comes when you can *declare* that you are one hundred percent responsible for your life and everything in it! I did not say that this is the truth. I am saying that it is something you can declare to gain power in your life. It becomes 'truth' because you say it is so.

I have to be honest; I almost edited that part out. I should have at least put "*trigger warning*!"

When I was first told the path to my happiness and freedom was in taking one hundred percent responsibility for everything,

I wanted to punch that person in the face! How absolutely stupid! You want me to take responsibility for what my ex is saying and doing? You want me to take responsibility for the way my coworkers are? Not only did that seem like a stupid idea, but it also seemed impossible and overwhelming. It was a *hard no* from me on that one!

Hear this, though; I did not say take '*fault or blame*.' I said, '*responsibility*.'

I take responsibility to give myself the power to alter the situation because altering the situation *matters to me*.

Just as believing you are a victim and life is happening to you, declaring you are one hundred percent responsible is a belief and a space to stand in your life. So why take that stand? Here is where I ask for a bit of trust and openness—not to believe me but trust in yourself to explore the idea.

I am not talking about the experiences of tragedy that happen, like the death of a loved one or a pandemic. Yet, in these cases, there is still something you can do. A change in mindset where you see life as happening *for* you will help you find the blessings and turn your world into a miracle. Ask yourself, what is the lesson here? What are the blessings? Tony Robbins says, what is wrong is always available to see, but so is *what is right*!

I cannot explain every example of how the world changes when I take one hundred percent responsibility, or this book would be thousands of pages long, but trust me that your world will alter when you do.

Life and people start to respond differently. Remember, so much of our life is patterns and habits. Our brains put part of us on autopilot, so we can focus on other things. I do not have to think about walking, so I focus on higher functioning needs. Consider that part of your autopilot might be your relationships and how you show up in them.

When I show up differently and get committed to a new outcome, a pattern is broken. And when the pattern is broken, the other person cannot help but show up differently too. By owning my responsibility, I bring a new way of behaving into the relationship and the way we relate to each other alters. Like changing up a step in a dance, now that dance looks different as your partner moves accordingly. It might not happen the first time or even the fifth time, but eventually, it will change. This is where your commitment is required. Sometimes we give up too quickly.

"I trained four years to run only nine seconds. There are people who do not see results in two months, give up and leave. Sometimes failure is sought by oneself." Usain Bolt

I remember when I applied this strategy to my relationship with my ex-husband. We were fighting over scheduling and how we both were *certain* the other person was being inconsiderate. We argued back and forth. I would storm away and cry, and he would hang up. We were both super confused and frustrated that the other person was not listening or understanding our point of view. Then it hit me. I said I would take one hundred percent responsibility for this relationship going well.

Ugh!!!

So I dug reeeeeally deep down into my toes and went back into the conversation from the space of *declaring* it was one hundred percent my responsibility to make this work.

I said, "It does not work for me that we are fighting. I have said that I would have a family that I am proud of where everyone is happy, healthy, whole and complete. And from that commitment, I want to understand you and who I am being for you that makes you feel taken advantage of." He grumbled in defence a bit more, and I stayed in my commitment to being responsible for understanding how he was experiencing me.

It took real strength to stop defending my point of view and to truly get his. I had to stop talking and listen. I had to say back to him what he had said, so he knew I heard him. And something super cool happened as he got the experience that I was hearing him and committed to knowing why he felt the way he felt. He started to express what he felt and what he needed so he could feel differently about the situation. It turned out that it was not about the time spent with kids, although I was certain that was his problem. It was that he needed a schedule to prepare and plan, or else his experience was of being at my beck and call.

For the record, that same situation was occurring differently for me. I felt he did not understand or care about my life and therefore did not want to help with *his* kids. Yet, how could he understand what I was up to? I had not communicated it.

I did not see that my belief of *'I am on my own in this new divorced life'* guided my actions and made me not communicate properly with him. I was not aware that subconsciously the payoff was that I got to be right. I was being right about my belief that he did not support me and that I was on my own. Ultimately what I wanted was a positive co-parenting relationship. Unconsciously, my need to be right was preventing that. You can be right or you can be loving, but you cannot be both at the same time. I had to give up being right to get to the results of being loving and having the relationship work.

We see what we believe!

In taking one hundred percent responsibility for the relationship and my experience, I was able to change the way I showed up. Eventually, I was able to make the situation work in the positive way I wanted. I got to have the results of a positive co-parenting relationship instead of being right about how 'selfish' he was being and how 'everything' was on me.

Responsibility is a gift that you give yourself!

What is something or someone in your life that you could start to see differently? What or who could you take one hundred percent responsibility for and try to understand better? How can you change the story you have about it? ____________________

____

____

____

I love Jim Rohn and how he tells it like it is. He says this about being responsible for one's own life,

"To attract better, you need to better yourself. Stop doing the same things and expecting change. Stop blaming others. Start transforming your mindset. Start upgrading your habits. Start being more positive. It is time to take responsibility for your reality."

CHAPTER SEVEN

None of it is Real

"Our past is a story existing only in our minds. Look, analyze, understand and forgive. Then, as quickly as possible, chuck it!" ~Marianne Williamson

What if I told you that none of what you believe is real?

What if I told you that everything that we see is a creation in our minds. A creation that is reinforced by the language we use and the people we enroll to support us in our beliefs. Consider that what you experience in your life and what you feel so emotionally attached to is simply a beautiful, or not so beautiful creation that started in *your mind.*

And here comes that R word again. Responsibility.

Having a life you love that fulfills you, will take being responsible. It will require you to take ownership of your life and to be who you are capable of being. You will need to let go of your certainties and your stories; how much mommy did or did not love you. Let go of what daddy said or did not say. Let go of all the ways you have been abandoned, abused, mistreated and neglected.

One of the best things I have heard on my journey:

"What happened to you was not your fault, but healing from it is your responsibility."

No matter where your experiences of life have led you to at this point, you have a choice now. When we know better, we do better. Having read this far in the book, you should now know your thoughts are creating your reality. The thoughts you allow into your mind create your feelings, your feelings dictate your actions, and your actions are the reasons for the results that you see.

I am going to say that again.

The thoughts you allow into your mind create your feelings, your feelings dictate your actions, and your actions are the reasons for the results that you see. Thus your thoughts are creating your reality.

Are you going to accept the responsibility for your life from this point forward?

Are you ready? Do you really want to be unleashed, totally fulfilled and fully self-expressed? Do you want to claim your space and contribution in the world? Right now! Starting today!

Then sit up straight, pump your arms up into the air and shout it out with me!

I am my *own* creation!

Say it over and over until you really hear it and feel that deep desire for the self and life that is waiting for you to lay claim!

I am my *own* creation!

An incantation I say every morning by Tony Robbins is, "Now I am the voice. I will lead, not follow. I will believe, not doubt. I will create, not destroy. I am a force for good. I am a leader. Defy the odds! Set a new standard! Step up! Step up! Step up!"

I remember when I started to understand that I was playing small and for the first time, I saw the limiting beliefs that were keeping me from playing big.

Like most of us, I was situated in a comfortable, safe space in the middle of the crowd. I fit in but I also wanted to *feel special.* I wanted to *be special.* I believed I was not disciplined, organized or smart enough to really excel and that I had to work hard for every bit of success I achieved. It was not clear to me that this idea was a limiting belief. That my work life was showing up that way because I believed it was true. I was certain that it was the truth about me and I felt stuck with this way of being.

When I finally saw my thoughts as limiting beliefs, I challenged them. I saw that it was not the truth, and I had many examples where I had been extremely disciplined, organized and smart. But because I had the thought that I was not disciplined, organized or smart enough, this created feelings of futility and hopelessness which resulted in me taking ineffective actions. I would be inefficient with my time and I would lack structure to my workdays. I was easily distracted and would forget stuff. I dropped balls and overcommitted myself constantly. I tried hard to make it work, but I was left feeling stuck and helpless.

At least I got to be right about who I was (insert eye roll here). See, I told you I was undisciplined, disorganized, and not smart enough - just look at my results! Or lack thereof. These thoughts became a pattern of behaviour. Then the results and struggle reinforced my limiting belief. Remember, a belief is just a thought you repeatedly tell yourself.

You know what smart stands for, right? Specific, measurable, attainable, relevant and time based.

I was not, not smart. I simply had not created a plan that was specific, measurable, attainable, and relevant, with time-based goals based on what I wanted. I showed up unprepared and lived into my beliefs and patterns. My story to myself was: I am not the type of person who can have massive success or effectiveness because I am not disciplined, organized or smart enough.

I was unhappy, stuck and felt like a failure, but I was right! Yay me! It was so difficult, almost impossible for me to show up any way other than disorganized and undisciplined. It got to the point where I was convinced I had ADHD or some other genuine focusing condition. And even if I did have ADHD or any other type of neurodiversity, I could still be successful and achieve my dreams. Limiting beliefs are simply limiting beliefs.

Once you see what is running you and truly understand that what you think is the '*truth*' is really a belief you are living into, you begin to be *free*! How much would you love to be truly free from anything limiting you and the happiness and fulfillment you experience in life?

Now can you see what I said earlier? You have thoughts, but you are *not* your thoughts!

So, if it is not the truth that I am undisciplined, disorganized and not smart enough, what could be true? Said another way, what could I replace that thought with? What would be possible for my life in the area of my work if I was free from these limiting beliefs? I can create whatever I want! *You can create whatever you want!*

Did you know that the brain cannot tell the difference between fantasy and reality? As long as something is at least fifty percent believable and declared with emotion behind it as if it is already happening, the mind will believe it. So pick a new story, get emotionally invested in it, and see what happens.

"Whatever the mind can conceive and believe, it can achieve!" ~Napoleon Hill

Here are some of the new empowering beliefs I created around who I am with regard to my career. I am smart, focused and clear! I take intentional actions daily that move me towards my goal! I am unstoppable! I have all the skills and tools necessary for explosive growth! I set clear intentions for my purposeful work! I show up consistently and with a clear, focused plan! I am beyond excited to show up in my work. I empower and develop others. I am able, capable and powerful!

When I created these empowering beliefs, I kept them alive by powerfully declaring them at the start of each day. Then I started to be different with my work. I was coming up with exciting, impactful ideas, finding great resources, and being consistent. I was using new tools and producing breakthrough systems and results. I shocked and surprised myself! I kept saying out loud, "Who *am* I?!?"

I would laugh, but the truth is I was surprised about who I was being. It was like a whole new world opened up to me once I stepped outside of the beliefs that had been limiting me in my career. Sidenote here: it did not happen overnight. It takes time to become the person you are creating, you have never been her before. Some days I would forget but I kept returning to this strategy until it became a new habit that I formed.

Could you imagine that anything you want for yourself and your life could be available to you?! Well, I am here to say it can be! And it starts *with you.* It starts with the thoughts you are telling yourself, whether consciously or not.

Where do you see you are fulfilling your beliefs? How are you getting the results that match up to what you are certain is true about you in that area? Remember that you are seeing it because you believe it. You can do this for every area but just pick one right now. Is it family, career, health, finances, self-care? Write out what your current beliefs are about this area. Be honest about what you see. Do not judge it or edit it. It is not about being right or wrong. It just is.________________________________

____

____

____

Now look at those beliefs and recreate them stated in a way that is empowering. I do not just mean the opposite of what you wrote but something new. If what you wrote above is not true, what could be true in this area that would light you up and get you excited about your life?__________________________

____

____

____

At the heart of our experience of life is our mindset.

Often we are suffering because we resist what is so about life. We believe that we are living a life that should not be happening, with people that should not be acting the way they are. We resist, and we fight to change them, us and life.

What if life is not about fighting what is currently happening but accepting it? Then we get to spend our energy working to build our new vision for our life.

It does not mean settling or tolerating abuse. (If you are unsafe, you need to acknowledge you are unsafe and get help). It does not mean accepting any bs thoughts that we create to let us off the hook for change. What I mean is we need to accept *what is* because it is *what it is* in this current moment. If we cannot accept our current life, if we cannot acknowledge our current life, we cannot grow from it. Think about the amount of energy and upset that you can save by focusing on what you are building instead of what you are resisting.

Where focus goes, energy flows.

When we are so focused on resisting, fixing, changing, doing more, doing better, doing different, we fail to see the opportunity and the miracle of life that exists right in front of us in this present moment. We fall into the 'when and then' paradigm. When x happens then I will be y. When I am thinner, I will wear that dress. When I achieve that job, I will consider myself a success. When he shows me more love and affection, then I will give it back. And on and on it goes.

What could happen in your life if you use that focus and energy that you have spent thinking about how to change or make things better or different and instead focus on what you want to create?______________________________

____

____

____

It is possible.

You can start today by choosing where to look. Choose what you want to give your attention, your focus and your energy to. Choose what you say to yourself about yourself, and what you say about your people and your life.

Ultimately, happiness is a choice.

There are things that we cannot alter, but we always have the choice of what to look at, what feelings we allow to stay, and what we choose to believe.

That choice is the choice between survival and aliveness.

Between surviving life and thriving in it.

Between feeling stuck and hopeless or empowered and fulfilled.

One choice will leave you resisting what is happening and feeling resentful and regretful. The other choice will leave you creating your life, free to be and act, grateful and present to the miracle of your life.

"Everything can be taken from a man (person) but one thing: the last of the human freedoms — to choose one's attitude in any given set of circumstances, to choose one's own way."
~ Viktor Frankl

(Austrian neurologist, psychiatrist, philosopher, author, and Holocaust survivor)

And here is an even more grandiose thought; do not stop at choosing what you give your attention to. Think about what life will look like if you actually commit to *being the change* you wish to see in the world.

When you find yourself thinking something or someone should be a certain way, what if you showed up that way? When you catch yourself thinking, my partner does not do nice things for me, what if you decided to do nice things for them? If you think, my children do not appreciate me, what if you were to ask yourself, how can I be an expression of appreciation whether that is to them or to myself.

What incredible access to power and happiness we have when we declare that we *are* the change we want to see. Commit to showing up every day as *I am the change I want to see*! When you find yourself complaining about the way something or someone is, ask yourself, how can I bring more of what I want to this situation? That is an ultimate place to take responsibility so you can alter anything in your life!

Speaking of altering anything, let's talk about what stops us sometimes. Do you have those areas in your life where you know what you need to do to make a difference but you do not seem to be making progress? You may even get started on a good path for a while, and then one day you wake up and realize you have stopped? Trust me, I know how frustrating it is when you cannot get to the bottom of why.

Let me go back a moment to the story about how I had altered how I was doing in regards to my career. By now, I had identified what limiting beliefs were holding me back and had created fantastic new empowering ones. I had set a structure in place for reminding myself of those empowering beliefs daily. I was also reinforced by seeing positive results show up. So why was I not consistent in doing the things I knew would make a difference?

Why did I find myself sabotaging myself and my results? Why was I still not showing up consistently?

When I got honest with myself about that, I saw that I did not want to be responsible for playing a bigger game of life. It was not that I did not want the results of thriving. It was that I did not want the *responsibility* of how I would need to *consistently* show up in my life, for myself and others. I said I wanted more, better, different and then when it was time to be that, I shrunk away and played small. I believed that *consistently* showing up was harder than not showing up. Now, there is a limiting belief!

You may have heard the phrase, "the devil we know is better than the one we don't." Not having the level of success I wanted was frustrating, discouraging and defeating, but staying the same was comfortable and familiar. I knew how to do what I was already doing. To take responsibility for my greatness and what I was capable of would require me to let go of my limiting beliefs. It required me to be consistently bolder and braver in ways that my old life never asked of me.

Developing the courage and discipline to create a new mindset and positive habits felt hard. But we all know living in frustration, discouragement, and defeat is hard.

Choose your hard.

Trust me, showing up consistently is way easier in the long run! And when you are consistent and disciplined, you create momentum that leads to mastery, new habits and your ultimate success and fulfillment.

Your growth starts at the end of your comfort zone. Are you ready to get uncomfortable? Are you starting to see what is available to you beyond those limits and your self-imposed ceiling?

Everything you want for yourself and your life exists outside that comfort zone.

"That was the day she made a promise to herself to live more from intention and less from habit."

CHAPTER EIGHT

Journey Into Self

"The privilege of a lifetime is being who you are."
Joseph Campbell

As I struggle to begin this chapter, I am up against what is called '*imposter syndrome.*' I like to refer to it as an even more common syndrome—self-doubt.

I see all the things that are being neglected as I focus on this book and I ask myself, "Am I doing the right thing?" "Who is going to read this anyway?" "You should be focusing on your health and weight release." (I don't like to call it loss because then I always try to find it.)

I started comparing myself to others. "Look at Erin sharing her workouts and clean eating on FB! She is killing it, and I am over here working out twice a week and eating popcorn for dinner." I hear myself saying, "You are a single mother. Get your head out of the clouds and focus on your paycheque and work!"

"Oh, Shanda promoted again! Wow, good for her! You are not the best at anything, hey?" And I hear a very loud voice say. "What. Are. You. Doing?"

I felt sick and wanted to cry. Now I know why they say your *why* is so important. It is what will pull you through your imposter syndrome or self-doubt.

To know why I wanted to launch a writing, speaking and coaching business at almost fifty, I did an exercise called 'Seven Layers Deep Why.' This exercise helps you get to why you want what you say you want. I was surprised by what I discovered about why I wanted to be brave and show up for you here.

What I saw started with wanting to help others, to share my lessons to help others alleviate and avoid pain. There was a little bit of wanting to be significant and to do something that matters. And of course, to prove I was worthy and could make something of myself!

Then I got emotional, and it hit me. I want to believe that all that pain and suffering I have experienced was for a reason — that my pain had purpose. I want to know myself as bigger than I have ever dreamed possible. That the abuse, rape, demeaning behaviour did not take the best parts of me! I knew that I have a gift to share inside me, and nothing or no one can take that gift! I also saw that I did not want to die never having stood bravely in the space of my big dreams!

I was certain that living a good life was available to me but I believed that I was not the type to have a *great life*. And then I got really emotional. It kills me to think of all the people's lives

I will not help make better. All the pain and suffering they are experiencing that I could help alleviate! I started to think of the people who would lose if I did not win in this life. Including myself!

I show up as my best self because being my best is also what is best for others. It is how I can make the biggest difference.

It is the same as you showing up as your best self, it is best for others too! How much of my own pain and suffering could have been alleviated if I knew then what I know now? If this book was put into my hands twenty or more years ago! This book, this showing up, this sharing is my gift to you in the hopes that your showing up happens soon rather than later.

What does showing up mean for you?__________________

____

____

____

What is that one thing that could be your gift to others?____

____

____

____

What would it feel like if your life's purpose was fulfilled?____

____

____

____

And yes, it is not just one thing that does this, but I am talking about *that one thing*. The one thing that whispers to you quietly from the depths of your heart that you maybe are not listening to. The book, the song, the business, the art, the contribution you know you have inside of you.

What is the one thing that by living into it and stepping into it bravely would make the world a more beautiful, happy, and loving place?____

____

____

____

I get why people give up! Believing in your goals and dreams can be hard. But remember, the pain of regret and your life's purpose unfulfilled is harder!

I recently heard that if you are really good at something, you are not growing. That if you never fail, you are not living a big enough life. Yeah so! Sometimes we need to rest in the little wins. I love to focus on what I am certain I am good at so I can get that little win and checkmark. The sense of accomplishment I get from checking those boxes on my to-do list fills my cup.

Although soon enough, there is this little voice inside me that says, "I want more." What if I could actually make a bigger impact in the world?"

Think about this. What if that dream and voice are there because you do have something to share? What if you are supposed to keep stretching and growing, conquering your self-doubt and limiting beliefs along the way?

Like great warriors, we fight for that quiet ache or possibility inside of ourselves that says, *I am* made for more!

One of my all-time favourite quotes that I have everywhere around me is this one from Marianne Williamson.

Our deepest fear is not that we are inadequate.
Our deepest fear is that we are powerful beyond measure.
It is our light, not our darkness that most frightens us.
We ask ourselves, " Who are we to be brilliant, gorgeous, talented and fabulous?"
Actually who are we NOT to be?
You are a child of God. Your playing small does not serve the world.
There is nothing enlightened about shrinking so that other people
won't feel insecure around you.
We were born to manifest the glory of God that is within us.
It is not just in some of us;
It is in everyone.
As we let our own light shine, we unconsciously give other people
permission to do the same.
As we are liberated from our own fear, our presence automatically liberates others.

Your playing small *does not* serve the world.

Those words run through my mind over and over as I see so many playing small. It makes me sad. Not just for them but for others because of the gifts and experiences we will be denied when someone does not own their greatness. What if Adele never stepped into her voice? What if Oprah stopped believing in herself? We would never have the gifts that they bring.

I want you to ask yourself what is the cost of not believing in yourself? What is the cost of not going for your dreams and of not investing the time and energy in creating life on your terms. What you have might be good and fine, but if you are reading this book, I am going to guess that you want more than *good and fine*.

What is it costing you in experiences, joy, fulfillment, relationships, accomplishments to not go for it? What is playing small with your life keeping from you?________________

____

____

____

When we think of playing big, it feels terrifying and often not even an option because we are certain that we are already playing full out. And in a way, we are. At least to the best of our beliefs. And our circumstances. Oh, and also our feelings.

Sometimes I tell myself that it is due to *other people* that I am not where I could be. Limiting belief alert! I will say it again. *You are responsible for your life*!

Somewhere along the way, as a culture, we adopted a way of believing that one must be humble and have a certain level of shame around acknowledgment. Especially women. Think about it, when a friend compliments you on a new dress, do you automatically say, "Oh, this old thing? I got it on sale." Or if someone says you look like you have lost weight or have been taking care of your health, do you say something along the lines of "Oh God no! I ate like such a pig last night." What about if someone tells you that you did a great job? Do you feel you have to tell them what a great job they did too? We call it being humble but consider it is one of the many ways we keep the lid on ourselves.

No more, I say! That bs ends today! Right here! Right now!

Living your best life and stepping into your greatness will take a willingness. It sounds like a simple thing. Like who would not want to be great and shine every day?! As I said before, when we are attached to our identity, altering or expanding that identity takes an intentional commitment. It can feel like stepping out of your skin. It can feel scary, like you might not survive. You fear that you might be made fun of or judged. Or it might be incredibly uncomfortable.

I had to give up '*crazy like a fox*' and '*good but just not good enough*' belief. I had to give up the fear that maybe I was wrong about being any kind of special. I had to stop worrying that people would laugh and say, "As if!" when I stretched out of my comfort zone.

Remember when I confessed to you that I am still quite hard on myself? Part of breaking through that is seeing that I had always put a limit on what I thought I was capable of. I wanted so badly to be special and valuable that I would work really hard to succeed. And that got me a lot of good things. But it came with a price and always a limit because I felt undeserving of anything beyond a certain level.

I had to work hard for everything I achieved. I was good, but I was not great. I had a good heart and was valuable to people, so I was good. I felt something was inherently wrong about me, as evidenced by things people had done and said to me, so I was not capable of being great. Or so I thought.

Have you ever had the experience that you are making progress and moving along on your goals, then something starts to slip? Maybe it is something tangible, but sometimes it is a mood shift or sudden lack of discipline and follow-through. A more common term is self-sabotage, but regardless of what you call it, the experience is a pullback on getting what you say you want.

I would say it felt like I took ten steps forward and eight back. I would still be making progress, but it was always a little short of the elusive goal that I wanted. I would try to comfort myself and say that where I landed was good enough, or I would pretend that I did not want the goal I had set out to achieve. "It is not really that important to me." or "I changed my mind. I do not really want that anyway." Sometimes I would blame it on my circumstances. Ultimately though, I was failing to break through a limit that contained me.

My weight is a great example of that. I have literally been around the same weight, give or take twenty pounds, no matter my approach. I stick to a workout or an eating plan, and I start to see great success and feel good about myself. And then I cannot even tell you what clicks, but something does, and I slip. I miss working out. I drop my commitment to my food plan and say, "Oh, it is just one meal. I will do better tomorrow." And with each choice, I hate what I am doing, and I get so mad at myself, but it is like I am powerless over the invisible force sabotaging me. I find it happens just as I am getting close to my next big mark. Then comes the shame, and I fall even more into the old behaviours that produce the old results. Crap!

Of course, I want to hit my health and weight-loss goal. I get how important that is for me as a mature mother living with diabetes. You would think I would be able to shame myself into losing weight or scare myself with the thought of losing limbs. But shame never works to produce long-term results! Let me say that again. *Shame nevers works*!

Yet, there was this powerful force that stopped me. No matter what I have achieved in my life or how successful I am in other areas, in this one area I seem to always struggle and fail.

Then I got really honest with myself. I had limiting beliefs about my health and weight-loss goals. "It will never happen, so why try. Nothing you do makes a difference. This is just who you are." In the creation process of life, it states that our thoughts (what we tell ourselves) lead to our feelings, and our feelings lead to the actions we take. Then the actions we take lead to the results we see. The minute I started to think, *nothing you do makes a difference*, and *it will never happen. You have never achieved it before. Why should it happen now?* I start to feel hopeless, sad, futile, defeated, and even angry. And with those feelings running me, I give up. I believe my thoughts, and the more times I fail in my weight loss goals, the more I believe my thoughts.

Remember, this is not a conscious process until you see it for yourself!

Tony Robbins talks about a thermostat we have set for our lives. It is a state of homeostasis that, physiologically and psychologically, we crave— the predictability and safety we need at a basic level. The belief that our world needs to occur as predictable and safe so we can avoid getting eaten by sabretooth tigers.

Your beliefs set that homeostatic temperature. Whenever I started to get close to the weight and body I wanted to have, I would get excited, but then my thermostat would kick in. I would start thinking, "Who do you think you are trying to be all fit and gorgeous? You do not deserve to have this too. You are an average temperature, not above average! Stay in your own lane!" Once I accepted that I was gorgeous regardless of my weight, my weight became about my health. Once I believed I deserved to be healthy, my weight started to come off on its own. I left the cycle of struggle behind when I changed my beliefs thus changing my actions.

Your actions will always be in direct correlation to how something occurs for you. Said another way, what you do is a direct reflection of how you think. You will take actions consistent with what you tell yourself.

In what area of your life does your thermostat keep getting reset? Maybe it is your health goals? Another common one is in your career or dreams. Sometimes it happens with our relationships. We want a loving, nurturing relationship but we have a limiting belief about what is possible in love.

Sometimes you may push through and achieve your goals, but there is a lack of joy and fulfilment once you get there.

In what area do you feel you keep getting pulled back? How does self-sabotage show up for you? There is no right or wrong answer; just look at your life and patterns. ________________

____

____

____

So what is it going to take to be able to make that choice for your happiness and empowerment? It starts with identifying and owning your unique gifts. Laying claim to what is special and unique about you and then being bold and brave enough to live into it.

If you cannot believe the good things about yourself or it feels too hard to come up with items for the list below, make it up! You have to be willing. Remember this fun fact: the brain cannot tell the difference between fantasy and reality. As long as something is at least fifty percent believable and declared with emotions to back it up, our brain believes us.

I am not asking you for the '*truth*.' I am asking you to declare positives about yourself! If you do not do this, that tells me that you are not willing to play a bigger game and provide love, acceptance and support inward. Nothing bad or wrong about that, but it does come with consequences. Imagine your own best friend not being able to find seven things that are great about you.

So give up the humility, give up the punishment, give up the shame, and step bravely right now into your greater self.

We are in this together, so come on, repeat after me, "I am willing, able and excited to acknowledge, declare and own my superpowers!"

Say it again with more feeling this time! "I am willing, able and excited to acknowledge, declare and own my superpowers!"

Girlfriend, let us list great things about you!

What is great about me is?______________________________

____

What is great about me is?______________________________

____

What is great about me is?______________________________

____

What is great about me is?______________________________

____

What is great about me is?______________________________

____

What is great about me is?______________________

____

What is super great about me is?__________________

____

I want you to boldly share what you have discovered are your superpowers. Do not downplay it or excuse it. Share it! My teenage daughter laughs at me all the time when I get in the car, look in the mirror and say, "I am really pretty!" Or sometimes, when I am proud of myself for what I have figured out, I will come to the kitchen and declare, "I am super smart!" I think she giggles because it is not common to hear people declare what they are great at and to acknowledge themselves. I am happy to be that example to a young woman growing up. One of my favourite sayings is, "We can't tell them; we have to show them." I cannot tell her to feel good about herself and to acknowledge and celebrate her gifts. I have to show her a woman who can do it!

Mothers, I especially want you to hear this as another reason it is so important to be the change you wish to see! Regardless of what you say to your children about how to be in the world, it is *what you do* that will have the impact. Like the quote says, "*who you are being speaks so loudly, I cannot hear what you are saying*."

Your job is to stand still inside and claim the power of who you are regardless of what life or people will have you believe you are. Lay claim to who you say you are. Acknowledge! Celebrate! And then share it with the world!! It is through your superpowers that our world will be saved! Start first, with saving yourself!

"I wish I could show you, when you are lonely or in darkness, the astonishing light of your own being." ~Hafiz

CHAPTER NINE

Weeds or Seeds

"What is planted in each person's soul will sprout." Rumi

If I told you your mind is the garden of your life, would you see that you have planted seeds or weeds? Outer reality is a reflection of inner reality. What this means is that the garden you see called your life is a direct reflection of what you have planted internally. Again, please do not hear that as you are bad and wrong if your garden of life is a little weedy. We want to see the weeds so we know where to start pulling and replanting.

Where do you see beautiful flowers in your life?__________

____

____

____

What are your thoughts about that area? What do you tell yourself in regards to the results that you see here?__________

____

____

____

Where do you see weeds in your life? __________________

____

____

____

What are your thoughts about that area? What do you tell yourself in regards to the results that you see here?__________

____

____

____

Tending a garden is an ongoing process. What happens if we do not weed a garden? All the beauty and possibility in it is overtaken by weeds as roots become strangled and cut off from the source of life. All the beauty is gone and all that is left is the memory of what was once possible in that space.

See yourself on your knees pulling weeds. All those limiting beliefs that you listed above pull them out one by one. Clear that garden. *Unbecome* everything that is not you. It does not matter what your story was nor all the years of *proof* you have held onto believing you are not good enough. The details are beside the point. If mommy did not love you enough, pluck it out. If what daddy said or did not say hurt you, pluck it out! Reasons or results. You choose! Right now! Right here! Choose a new story. Your parents had their story. Do not make it your story. Pluck the thought that no longer serves you. The ones that you have told yourself over and over until you believed them, lived into them and proved them right. Pluck them! Let it go! You choose! Right here! What do you say is right?

Pull out, '*I am unlovable.*' Pull out, '*I am not good enough.*' Yank '*I cannot do it.*' Weed them all! "*I am not capable.*' *No one appreciates me.*' '*I am on my own.*' '*I don't belong.*' Pull out every last one that does not serve your greater self!

What weeds (limiting and disempowering beliefs) did you pull? What limiting beliefs are you choosing to stop listening to?

____

____

____

____

See, there is space now in your garden.

It is the beginning of a new opportunity for planting good stuff. The weeds were not wrong or bad. They were taking up space where the beauty of the flowers you want to enjoy throughout your life could be planted and bloom.

This book is not about planting some beautiful seeds (thoughts) once and thinking they will flourish. It is about always being the gatekeeper and gardener of our minds. You need to be conscious and focused on what you feed your mind. Unfortunately, the default conversation in our world is often one about all the things that are going wrong. To protect your new garden (mindset), start watching the conversations that you are a part of. Start watching what you are contributing to and engaging with inside your mind and out in the world with others.

When I first became the gatekeeper of my mind, I was surprised to see how much work it took. It was my natural inclination to complain and be negative which shocked me because I thought I was a positive person. Often I did not even realize I was doing it until after I left the conversation. I would be driving home or sitting there feeling *blah* or *ewww* about who I had been in that conversation.

I recently heard something that I try to hold in front of me as I go through my days and interactions with people. That is, leave everyone with the experience of being elevated. From that, I started to set an intention for everything, especially in my interactions with people. I do not always succeed, but I have succeeded more than I had in my past. It is quite natural to fall into the default conversation of '*what is wrong here.*' Creating something intentional and new takes work. I can promise you though, it gets easier and more natural as you bring it into your consistent way of being. There is also the added bonus of leaving you with the experience of being elevated, fulfilled and true to yourself.

"The most beautiful people we have known are those who have known defeat, known suffering, known struggle, known loss, and have found their way out of the depths. These persons have an appreciation, a sensitivity and an understanding of life that fills them with compassion, gentleness and a beautiful deep loving concern. Beautiful people do not just happen. ~Elisabeth Kubler-Ross

Recently, I went to visit someone very important to me. I often leave my interactions with her feeling a little inauthentic, feeling like I was more focused on impressing her and being seen as smart than I was on enjoying our time together. Knowing that this is often how I leave the conversation with her, I set an intention for connection and collaboration. I also set an intention to leave her with an experience of contribution and being elevated. It was an inspiring and fulfilling experience. She even took notes on some of the things I shared! Not *trying* to be smart and impress her, I had been able to authentically contribute to her.

Another example of a powerful way I have used intention to create something I am proud of was during my divorce. Thankfully at that time, I had an amazing coach in my Landmark Worldwide Personal Development work. Sheryl Pearson gave me, or shall I say, helped me create what guided my divorce and made it a more positive experience for all involved. I was declaring how hard I knew it was going to be and how bad my life would turn out after my husband left and she stopped me. She said, "Brandy, you decide and declare right now how *you say* it is going to go!" Now I see that she was using the power of intention. Thankfully I did what I was told!

At that moment, I set my intention: I would have a family I am proud of, where everyone is happy, healthy, whole, and complete! This was so important to me because there were moments when my emotions ran high and I felt stuck in my victim story. How I was going to get through my divorce did not seem clear. Through the tears and the fighting, I would catch myself and remember my intention. "I will have a family I am proud of where everyone is happy, healthy, whole, and complete!" Having that intention pulled my behaviour towards what I wanted and away from my anger and sadness. It had me take actions that ensured happy, healthy, whole, and complete were available for all of us.

"Even in the dark soil, a seed is becoming something beautiful." ~Mary Davis

CHAPTER TEN

Moving Out

"Talking about our problems is our greatest addiction. Break the habit. Talk about your joys."

~Rita Schiano

Just like we have done throughout the book with becoming aware of our thoughts, it is important to do this with our emotions as well. Like I said in Chapter Two, we have an emotional home that we consistently return to. An emotional state we are familiar with and that we find comfort in, especially during challenging experiences. It is an automatic response, much like the fight or flight response. Our emotions are a habit we have developed and strengthened with our consistent behaviour. Sometimes we give them more power than being a habit as we tell ourselves that there must be a reason they exist.

When I experienced upset, I used to go to shame which led to beating myself up. I would be really mean to myself. I would say terrible things in my head that I would never have spoken to my worst enemy. Things like, "You are such a loser!" "Why do you think anyone would care!" "Of course you failed!" "I am so embarrassed for you!"

I think I believed that if I was going to be hurting, I should be the one doing the hurting. It brought a false sense of control. I guess I thought that if I caused it, I would also be able to make the pain stop. The problem was that I started to believe the awful things I would say to myself. It was lonely, it was sad, and it was a painful emotional house to live in. But it was also comfortable because it was familiar.

To free myself from this habitual behaviour of returning home to shame, I first needed to identify it. Then I had to see it when it was happening, and change my thoughts to ones that would lead to a new feeling. That did not happen overnight. Changing emotional habits takes awareness and practice.

What is the emotional house that you live in? The space that you come back to in moments of uncertainty, discomfort, rejection or challenge. That home for me was shame and sadness. Living with clinical depression since I was a child, sadness and shame was a space I knew well. It was predictable and familiar, which made me comfortable in a weird way. Although living with these feelings was not pleasant nor what I would say I consciously wanted, it had become home.

In challenging moments, I would return home to shame and sadness and fall into feeling bad about myself. I struggle to understand if it was partly to gain some sense of power and control over how I was feeling by being the cause of it or if it were simply that I knew *how to do sadness*. I genuinely felt so much shame about who I was and the things I did and said. As I have mentioned, there was always this sense of not being good enough and needing to do better.

Remember, I believed that I did not matter and that the world was confusing. Those thoughts led to these feelings of shame and sadness. These feelings resulted from that early belief that I had formed when I was six and continued to influence everything until I finally *saw* them at forty-seven!

Look for yourself, what is the common emotion that occurs for you in times of challenge or upset? What do you consistently experience? Or look back at Chapter Two and the thoughts that were formed from your identifying experience, what emotion follows that thought?______________________________

____

____

____

Remember, our thoughts create how we feel and how we feel dictates the actions that we take. Then the actions you take are the reason you have the results you have. Step one is to see and get a hold of your thoughts and limiting beliefs so you can turn them into more empowering ones that will work for you not against you.

All of our emotions come from the meaning we give to events

and circumstances. Said another way, all our emotions come from our thoughts about the event and *what we say it means*.

Events have no inherent meaning. Meaning is always created in the mind. In *your* mind, and as a human being, we often do not give empowering meanings to events, others and ourselves. You must separate your meaning from what is happening.

On of the first distinctions that is explored at Landmark Worldwide is that there is what *happened,* and then there is the *meaning we give* to what happened.

The story we tell plays a big part in how we respond and act. '*He closed the door'* versus '*He slammed the door'* communicates two different scenarios. Sidenote: be responsible for the words and language you choose when relaying stories of events to yourself and others.

Part of the process of turning limiting beliefs into empowering ones is asking yourself, "what meaning *did I give* and what other meaning *could I give*?" There is no one reality. You create your reality with the meaning you assign. This is an empowering concept to understand.

"She realized none of it was real and set herself free."

Step two is to master your emotional state.

When you see yourself fall back and retreat into your emotional home, do not judge yourself. Do not blame yourself. Simply go there, reach out your hand and bring yourself back to being present and responsible in the moment. It is important to be kind when moving yourself out of your old emotional home. When we are in the familiarity of that home, we lose perspective on what is real. We make things *seem* worse than they are. Through the filter of our limiting beliefs, intense emotions arise, and we make our situations more challenging and messy.

In my emotional home of sadness and shame, there is a lot of dramatic crying and theatrics. I would really sink into that upset. The sadness and shame would manifest in me physically to the point that you simply had to look at me, and you could see how absolutely broken I felt.

One of the most transformational moments in altering my emotional home came from that same coach, Sheryl Pearson. I knew in my heart that my marriage was about to be over. As I was talking to Sheryl on my way home to see my husband, I was crying and screaming, "My marriage is over!" Sheryl cut me off and said, "Brandy! Get a hold of your drama! It is ruining your life!"

I was shocked she said that to me! I was also smart enough to hear it.

It took a few weeks before her words settled in and before I could see that I was attached to my emotional house of sadness and shame. Finally I could see that it was not serving me. Instead, it was limiting my ability to see reality. I was able to see what Sheryl had meant. My drama *was* ruining my life. And even worse, it was hurting everyone who cared about me.

Soon after, my husband had moved out, and I was in it deep and dark. I was not only in my emotional house of shame and sadness; I was in the freaking basement! One evening, I was in the kitchen with my oldest daughter cooking. As usual, I was fighting to hold back my tears. I was feeling heavy and hopeless and was being very dramatic about it. One look at my body language, and you could feel it. I was emphatically telling her how I was going to quit a course I was currently taking. I was giving her a long list of reasons why I was not capable of continuing because of what I was going through. She started to cry and said, "But Mom, why would you quit? You love this course."

At that moment, I stopped and saw the hurt my drama was creating for her and for me. Because she loves me so much, it hurts her to see me sad and down. I heard Sheryl's words again, "Brandy! Get a hold of your drama. It is ruining your life!" What Sheryl did not say was that my drama also was hurting the lives of anyone who loves me. At that moment, I committed to being stronger than I felt and made being strong and positive my biggest priority! Not just for *my life* but for *my girls, my friends, my sister and my parents*! For anyone and everyone. I realized that how I showed up for myself in life was also how I showed up for everyone else. How you do anything is how you do everything!

I did not know how I was going to be stronger or how I was going to stop forty years of the habits of shame and sadness. But I was super clear about the why! If I did not move out of my emotional house of sadness and shame and get a hold of my beliefs and patterns, I would ruin my life. Even worse, I would hurt the lives of the people I loved.

And do you know how you do it? How you start to move out of your old emotional house. You make the next *right* step. A single step. The next *right* choice towards what you do want and away from what you do not want. Life can be tough. Sometimes we can trick ourselves into thinking that is what it is always going to be. But nothing lasts forever. It is not going to be hard forever. If you take one step, and then another, and another, all of a sudden, you will find you are no longer in that darkness.

Some days my commitment to being positive and strong would be telling myself to just get out of bed. Then my next *right* step would be telling myself to get in the shower. Then to go make breakfast. Now fold the laundry. It was literally that simple.

Just. Keep. Moving.

I would talk myself step by step through the next *right* thing. The shame and sadness were still there, but I would not stop and unpack there. Acknowledge your pain but do not give your pain your voice! You have pain, but you are not your pain. You are so much more!

To break through my shame and sadness spiral, I had to understand that part of the reason that I would go there was my unconscious desire to win. When you are stuck in certain behaviours or habits, it helps to ask yourself, "What is the payoff?" You say you do not want the situation the way it is, but if you are not making the necessary changes to alter it, you need to ask yourself why? Human beings do things to seek pleasure or avoid pain. The payoff for our behaviour is often within these motivators. One common payoff in our behaviour is getting to be *right* and making the other person *wrong.* We get to dominate others and avoid being dominated. We get to *win* and avoid *losing*. But what are we winning?

Drama was one of the strategies I was unconsciously using to unsettle others and '*win.*' My payoff was avoiding being dominated and getting to feel a sense of dominance. Having gone through experiences of sexual assault, being dominated feels like certain death to me. And that feeling has not gone away, I am just more aware when I start to feel powerless or when I start to exert dominance. When I see my behavior clearly, I take responsibility for myself and my actions in these situations.

Another thing that made a huge difference was seeing what I call my '*chief operating system.*' The key statement that runs through me in moments of perceived rejection, hurt and embarrassment. Mine is, "Fuck you! You won't win!" It results in me engaging in drama, sadness and shame. If someone has done something that I perceive as hurtful, embarrassing or rejecting, this thought of "you won't win!" takes over. I do things that show such extreme sadness and shame so they cannot possibly '*win*' in the situation. I make it very clear that they are the cause of my suffering. This drama is also an unconscious test to see how much they care about me. The more upset and hurt that they are by my sadness, the more they care. I always got a weird sense of satisfaction out of that. Or if they are not someone close to me, I obsess about conversations I could have or things I could do to make them lose. I do not often take action but I spend a lot of time and energy having fantasy conversations and scenarios run through my mind.

These are hard truths to admit, but I do not want to live in sadness and shame. I am weeding my garden.

Everything comes with a cost! I got clear about the cost of my drama, and it motivated me to become responsible for managing it. Being responsible and managing the ways we wound up is all we can do as these habitual ways of being are not going anywhere. Remember, you are not broken or needing to be fixed. You have ways of being that were formed when you were young and they might not work for your life anymore.

Look at the habitual behaviours and ways of being that are not serving your life. Now, look at what they are costing you. Get real with yourself and look!

How much love is lost when you need to be *right* and make someone else *wrong*? Is there an impact on your health? Is there a sense of power and winning when you make everything about dominance to avoid being dominated?________________

____

____

____

I found myself avoiding people with different opinions or ways of life because I would feel inferior around them. Or if someone close to me had something to say about what I could or should be doing, I would get super defensive and dramatic. I could not see they were caring enough to share with me. I heard that I was doing it 'bad and wrong.'

Do your habitual behaviors stop the contribution of others and learning in your life because you refuse to give space for other perspectives?______________________________

____

____

____

I would not say certain things if I thought I would lose or look stupid. I was limited in my authentic expression of myself. When you are focused on winning and not losing, how is your self-expression limited? How are you limiting others?______________________________________

____

____

____

"You cannot wait until your life is not hard anymore before you decide to be happy." ~Nightbirde

Do you know why it matters to master your emotions? If you can only experience positive emotions when your external circumstances are ideal, you will always be a victim to life.

You want to feel positive emotions on the inside regardless of what is going on in your outer world. We cannot control what is happening, but we can control our focus and thoughts and what feelings we produce with them. Ask yourself, can I feel good even when things are hard?

If you were to start right now in creating a new emotional world for yourself, what would it be? Mine was strength and positivity. Some suggestions for you are joy, confidence, lightness, peace, calmness, happiness, honest, grateful, loving. Any quality is available to you. Create it now. You can change or add to it later but choose a quality or two right now.______

____

____

____

Here are six simple steps to developing emotional mastery.

1. Identify what you are feeling. I mean really feeling.

2. Acknowledge and appreciate your emotions and know that they are supporting you. Never make them wrong as they are here to serve you. Hold space and have grace for yourself. Negative emotions are teachers. Your life is speaking to you. Are you listening?

3. Get curious about the message the emotion is giving you. Connect to your feelings.

4. Get confident. You have had the emotions that you want before. The fastest way to an emotion is to remember a

time when you felt that emotion. This lets you feel it now. You have to be willing to change what you are focusing on and experience the emotion you want. I get that it can be tough to talk yourself out of an emotion that you have clung to or habitually talked yourself into, but get connected to the why and then move on to what you want to feel.

5. Plan for the blips. Develop or create certainty that you can handle things anytime they pop up. Think ahead and ask yourself, "How can I solve these things if they come up?"
6. Get excited and take action! Nothing happens in life without action. Practising mastering your emotions is what will have you actually mastering them.

It takes time to develop habits on the emotional level, just like it does on the physical level. I promise you though, this is one area you genuinely want to commit to mastering.

Remember you are picking some new flowers to put in your cleared-out garden. Make your life a beautiful garden full of all the lovely things you have consciously chosen for it!

"Your life is your garden. Your thoughts are the seeds.
If your life isn't awesome,
you've been watering the weeds."

CHAPTER ELEVEN

Watch Your Mouth!

"As was his language, so was his life" ~Seneca

Language is *everything*!

The world as we know it only exists to us because we have the language to describe it. A cup is a cup because we say it is. Otherwise, it would just be a vessel that holds liquid and that we drink from. "Cup" is the language that we use to create the world of a vessel that holds liquid. Our world exists in language. I think it is one of the most underestimated tools for creating our experiences in life. Start to watch what words you use and the experiences within you that follow your language. If you listen to yourself, you can direct yourself.

Think about when you say things like, "I am so busy!" Or how about "I feel overwhelmed." What about "I hate that!" What are the emotions that followed each of those statements?

Do you see how speaking this way creates an experience with challenging emotions and a change in your body language? Try it now. Say these sentences out loud and see what happens inside you?

Now try this, "I have an abundant life!" Or "I am super excited about everything that I am up to!" Or "I trust myself and my life!" What are you experiencing now? Do you notice your face feels lighter? Maybe your chest is up, your breathing deeper. Do you feel more capable?

We may think that our words are describing reality, when in fact, we create our reality with the words that we use. Language matters!

Think about how important paying attention to your language is. We spend the most time listening to ourselves. What goes in must come out. I could write a whole book on the power of language! For now, let me give you some key areas to pay attention to in how language shapes your world.

Watch when you say things like, "I *have to or need to* work on that." When you say "have to", it creates a feeling of burden and your mind hears that there is something you should put off. You sabotage your progress with that language. The minute something becomes a '*have to'* all the joy is gone. It creates a state of feeling heavy and bad or guilty if you are not doing it. Switch those words with '*want'* or '*get to'* and see how it feels. Or even more empowering, bring your why or intention into the statement.

Some of my favourite empowering and manifesting statements are "I am so happy and grateful that I am..." Or "How exciting that I am now..." Even "I am having the best time now that..."

Try it on. What is a common '*have to*' in your life? Switch it with *'want to'* or '*get to*.'

"I have to work out." Verses "I get to work out." "I need to be more organized." Or "I want to be organized because it makes my life easier!" "I have to clean the house." Or "I love having a clean, welcoming home for myself and my family." "I have to pick up the kids" or "I get to go grab my babies, which I love because it gives us time to connect and talk!"

Try it with your have to(s):

Disempowering language	Empowering Change

As well, when you use the word *'should'* whether speaking about yourself, others or the world, you are limiting potential. Do you remember when I talked about how we suffer when we think people and situations should be different than they are? When you use the word '*should*,' you are engaged in judgment of yourself and/or others. You are resisting life as it is and will be frustrated, angry or upset as a result. There is no winning when we judge. It keeps you stuck instead of focusing on new actions that will lead you to where you want to be. Remember that feeling happy and fulfilled comes with focusing on creating the new versus resisting current circumstances. Stop *shoulding* on yourself and others!

You also want to watch the way *you* language *yourself*. Be so super intentional about what follows the words '*I am.*' For what follows, '*I am'* is what you will become! We hear ourselves constantly affirming and declaring who we are or who we are not. Your words can put you back in that box, locked into a self-prescribed limiting identity that steals your freedom.

Try this instead, "In the past, I have been hard on myself." "It has been common for me to procrastinate and not plan my work." "Up until now I have been anxious about that." Try it with statements you commonly use to describe yourself that may be limiting you. Even if it is still a behavior that you are engaged in today but want to change, start with language and stating it as a past behavior. Stop affirming it as who you are and what you do in the present.

In the past, I have________________________________

____

It has been common for me to____________________

____

Up until now, I ____________________________

____

I try to reserve '*I am'* for the ways of being and experiences I want to live into in my life. I am bold and brave! I stand powerfully in my purpose! I love choosing healthy food to nourish my body! I am active and make positive choices daily for my body and mind!

Create a few empowering '*I am*' statements for yourself. And if '*I am*' feels hard to believe, start with "I am becoming the type of person who…" ______________________________

____

____

____

Having a great list of empowering statements can be a powerful tool to focus on in your life. I also recommend having a list of words or phrases that you *will not use*. This helps to ensure that you will not create a negative, challenging world for yourself. And please, please, please stop the '*it is hard*' or '*I cannot do it*.' Because if you say it is so, then you will be right.

You create your own reality.

Another one to watch is the '*when*' and '*then*' paradigm. Things like, "When I lose twenty pounds, I will be happy." Or "I just need to get through this age, and then it gets better."

Do not wait for someday to be happy and fulfilled. Your life is happening at this very moment!

'*When*' is right now! '*Ready*' is a lie. If we feel '*ready*' then we are not growing, and anything not growing is dying. Can you imagine if the only thing to have changed in your life on your next birthday is your age?

You also want to learn to control your emotional triggers even when you are alone.

Focus on who are you being in *all moments*? Mastery becomes easier when you practise it in all areas and are consistent. Language is important! If you say things like, "I am overwhelmed" or "I am so tired," that shows you do not have control over your emotional house. It shows me that you may be unpredictable or struggle to follow through with what you have promised.

Are you beginning to see that *you are the source*? You, my dear, are so powerful that *you can create your whole world with your thoughts and words*! Let that sink in.

I am powerful, able, and capable of creating the life I want!

You are meant for this moment! You are enough for the situation! In this very moment, you have the opportunity to call into being your Greatest Expression of Self.

Everything that has ever been calling to you can be yours. Your garden is weeded, and you are ready. You can now receive the truth that *you are the source of your life*.

You are love.

You are abundance.

You bring the beauty.

You are vitality and health.

You are everything you want to be and give to the world!

There is nothing wrong here and nothing wrong with you. You are not what you have been told. You have walked the journey that you were meant to walk and that journey has brought you here.

Now it is time to dive into something greater. Something deeper and more expansive for yourself and your life.

"I AM. Two of the most powerful words, for what you put after them shapes your reality!"

CHAPTER TWELVE

The Gift of Responsibility

"Regardless of what situations or circumstances you find yourself in, you are always responsible for the way you choose to respond to them." Drs. Ron & Mary Hulnick

Earlier I told you that what happened to you is not your fault, but healing from it is your responsibility. Let's look at that further.

I was very young when I got my Victim Badge. I do not know the exact moment, but it just feels like I have always felt like a victim. Like life was happening to me harder and faster than I could handle. My mom used to say, "God never gives us more than we can handle," and I remember answering, "I just wish he didn't trust me so much!"

I used to wear my Victim Badge with extreme pride. I had mastered telling all of the stories that went along with creating a world in which I was a victim. I was not even aware of what I was doing or aware there was any harm in it. I was simply sharing stories about things that had happened to me. I was actually kind of proud of what I had survived. The reaction from others of shock, then sympathy followed by their admiration when they saw that I was still standing, served to reinforce my desire to share the stories and identify with them.

I wish someone had come along then and told me that, yes, all those things had happened, but reaffirming them was keeping me powerless in my life.

I wish they had told me that standing in the space of being a sexual assault survivor, having been suicidal and living with clinical depression, having an abusive boyfriend, and many more traumatic experiences were not what defined me. They happened, but I was the one allowing them to continue to take from me without acknowledging that I was more than these stories.

We are so much more than the hard things we have gone through.

I see now that I wasted so many years and so much potential by being stuck in the story of those experiences. I was allowing a limited number of stories to define who I was. So much healing and freedom come from acknowledging that yes, they happened but they are not who we are. You must value and honour yourself regardless of what traumatic experiences happened in the past. And definitely not because of them. You are so much more than the tough things you have been though.

I want to give you the chance now to give up your story about the experiences that may have defined you up to now. What do you see would make a difference to let go of? Those defining experiences, although they happened, they are not who you are.

____

____

____

____

After letting go of the idea that these experiences from the past had defined me, I was able to look at them objectively. What I saw was the lessons and gifts that came from going through them.

What if life was happening for you and not to you?

What if all the things that we have gone through were to give you an opportunity to grow, stretch and deepen into the greatest version of yourself? When you realize that your old path was filled with lessons that helped you grow roots, you will begin to see your new path as abundant and filled with opportunities for self-expansion.

If you look back on some of the tough stuff in your life, there are two things I want you to see.

First of all, your amazing strength and resiliency has brought you to where you are standing today. Think about it. Your track record for surviving the tough experiences that you have been through is one hundred percent or you would not be here.

The second thing is to see the gifts that came from those experiences. This requires you to be incredibly responsible for your healing. You must first let go of how you have previously narrated your story to yourself about what happened. Then pull out the positives. They are there. There are no experiences that are all bad. Every experience has positives. You know what they say; every cloud has a silver lining. It is up to you whether or not you see the silver linings in your own life.

Choose your *hero* story over your *victim* story.

The breakdown in your life is what is creating you as an authority for that experience. If you are in a breakdown right now, this is not your whole story. It is only one part of it, and it is the part that will make you an authority on how to get through this. The minute you identify with the breakdown as the whole story and decide that this is who you are, you make a subconscious agreement to stay stuck. Do not buy into the breakdown. Do not let the emotional struggles take you into being a victim.

You are so much more than a breakdown or a victim story!

Remember that seeing what is '*right*' is always available? It is your choice about how you look at situations and experiences. You choose what you tell yourself, the meaning you give, and the language you use. You create the world with your language.

I chose to see that going through experiences of sexual assault helped me develop an incredible resiliency and a passion for empowering women. I choose to see the good, and the good is the truth because I say it is so. Declaring there were positives from the experiences, helped me find the silver lining, which also helped me to heal and move on. It brought me peace.

What are some positives that you can see out of the tough experiences you have been through? Do not give up if it is not clear right away. I will be honest. Mine was not clear either until

I started writing this chapter. As you look for what became a blessing, remember that everything is a creation. Your truth is your creation. It is not about it being *the truth* but about you *choosing to see it as the truth*?____________________________

____

____

____

It is important to get real not only about the things we say we want but also about why we might *not* want them. I know that sounds like a contradiction, but it is important to be aware that while you say you want something, there might be other thoughts stopping you.

Think of an area in your life that you would like to improve?____

____

____

____

What are some of the reasons you may not want success in this area? It does not always make sense but write what comes up.____

____

____

____

For me, it is my health and body goals. I kept repeating, "Nothing works!" and "It is not possible for me to reach my health and body goals." But if I get really honest, I avoided taking the responsibility to create and follow a specific plan for the long term. Then not only do I get to be right, but I also do not have to do the work it will take.

If it is what I truly want, I can end the whining, complaining and pretending that change is not possible. Getting real about the bs conversation of, "Oh poor me, nothing I do works. I eat healthy most of the time and still cannot lose weight!" Well, between you and me, I did not take the actions that would make a long-lasting difference. I did not want to admit that either. It is easier to be a victim of my metabolism, age and diabetes than to get real and develop the discipline and commitment necessary.

When we begin to be honest with ourselves, we begin to own the power we have to create the results in our lives. We stop pretending that we are powerless and that life is happening to us. Our actions are in direct relation to how we think about something. Said another way, we take actions based on what we believe is possible. When I got real about my victim mentality and ditched the belief that a healthy lifestyle and weight goals are not possible, suddenly, as if by magic, I started to take actions that made a difference towards my goals.

I am freed from my '*poor me'* victim story. I have my power back. Ultimately, happiness is not even about results or situations. It is about wanting to be empowered in your life. It is about being able to control your thoughts and your feelings so that you are not a ragdoll being tossed around from circumstance to circumstance. It is about liking and trusting yourself so that you are not at the mercy of others' opinions or actions. It is about being the author of your life and living a life you love on your *own terms*.

What do you see are some reasons that you might not want to do what it takes to get what you say you want? Just between us, what are you pretending is not possible for your life? Where are you telling yourself that you are stuck?________________

____

____

____

Awesome job looking at yourself and being honest!

Now keep going and write down what the '*truth*' is. When I was being honest, I told you that I could see I was not taking the actions that would make a difference. I was not following my meal plan. I would sneak bites of my girls' leftovers or a handful of chips or a cookie. If I did not track it, it did not matter, right? I worked out five times a week, one week, and then went on to say that is what I did. Although if I look back, one week it was three, one week it was two and rarely was it the five workouts that I had committed to. This is not about shaming myself or being made to feel wrong or bad. It is about being honest with myself so that I can have access to seeing new effective actions that will get me what I want.

Facing our truths is about getting real so we can have authentic power in our lives. It is about being able to count on ourselves for the truth and know that we are not victims to a weight scale that does not move, slow metabolism or even a bad partner. Maybe, just maybe, the 'problem' is not out there. Maybe, just maybe, it is that we are not telling the truth about what we do and what we do not do that is contributing to the situation or relationship going the way it goes.

What is the truth about what you are doing in this area? In service to yourself and your growth, be honest and get real. No shame.____

____

____

____

The title of this chapter is called, *The Gift of Responsibility.* Remember what I said earlier when I was first introduced to the idea of responsibility as a thing to take on in my life? I told you how angry I got. You may find it funny that I now call it a *gift.*

Taking responsibility for one hundred percent of your life and your relationships is a gift you can give yourself because that is the only way you have any power to make a change.

If I am certain that something is *happening to me* or that the problem is *over there* with the other person, I am powerless to produce a different outcome because I cannot control anything or anyone else. When I take one hundred percent responsibility, I can now find ways to make the situation or relationship work.

Hear me! I did not say fault or blame. I said choose to stand powerfully in declaring responsibility so that you have the power to access new solutions.

An empowered way to be in a relationship with others is to declare one hundred percent responsibility for how the interactions and relationship develops. Said another way, be the change you wish to see in the world. If you want more love in your relationship, ask yourself how you can be more loving? If you do not feel you get the respect you deserve, ask yourself who you are in regards to respect for yourself and others. You might also need to ask yourself why you are choosing to stay in a relationship that is not respectful.

This can be tough because we have mostly been raised to see relationships as fifty/fifty. When you think about it, though, that is weird. How would you be able to define where the fifty percent cut-off is? This becomes a much more complicated and tough way to do life and relationships. We often end up spending a lot of our time justifying, defending and explaining ourselves and our feelings and making sure they are doing their fifty percent. We say things like, "That is not my job!" Or, "That was your responsibility," or sometimes, "It is your fault we do not connect. You never make me feel special." A little aside here about empowering and disempowering language, never say "they make me feel…" I hope it is clear to you by now that you are the only one who makes you feel anything.

As hard as it can be with certain people in certain situations, I find immense power and joy in taking one hundred percent responsibility. Often in this space, I learn a thing or two about myself. I often have to ask myself, "Who am I being that this person occurs to me as cold or uncaring?" Sometimes I see that I have an unspoken certainty or viewpoint about them that subconsciously or energetically may be getting in the way. And sometimes, I learn that it is because of my limiting thoughts that I see the person's behaviour a certain way.

I remember when I realized I had the deep-seeded thought, '*I do not matter.*' The very next day, my boyfriend and I were driving back from our lake place, and he was sharing a story about how he had told the neighbours he would be back the following weekend. He said, " I do not know what the kids and Brandy are doing, but I am coming back." I was instantly upset. It felt like a slap in the face. I was filtering what he said through my belief that '*I do not matter*' and seeing everything as evidence of that. Through that filter, I heard, "It does not matter what Brandy is doing because she does not matter to me."

But that is not at all what he said.

Once I caught the thought, I could step outside of it. I could hear that he was saying how much he enjoyed the place. From there, I got curious about him and asked, "Tell me more about what it is that you love so much." We ended up having a great discussion about work stress, and I got to understand what life is like for him. That interaction went a very different way than it had in the past, where I would have been instantly hurt by his statement if I still believed I did not matter. And of course, because he did not really say that, he would have been confused and felt like he was made to feel wrong, once again.

Do you have anyone you are in a relationship with who feels like they cannot win with you? There might be a limiting belief operating there. Eventually, people may give up in relationships where they are always made to feel wrong. Remember, you can be right or be loving.

How great would it be to get responsible for what is in you that makes life feel so hard? Would you love to have the people you care about feel like they are heard and allowed to win? Can you see how empowering it would be to be free to express yourself and not wonder what happened? To get responsible for how you hear stuff? Start to look at where you could play around with declaring yourself one hundred percent responsible. Make it a game and have fun with it! See what new results you can create!

I am committed to taking one hundred percent responsibility in the following areas____________________________

____

____

____

Responsibility is a gift of power for yourself that alters outcomes, happiness, peace of mind, and so much more when you declare it to be yours!

"The moment you accept responsibility for everything in your life is the moment you gain the power to change anything in your life."

CHAPTER THIRTEEN

False Evidence Appearing Real

"Don't let the fear of what could happen, make nothing happen."

Do you remember when you were a kid, and *everything was possible*? You could be anything. There were no limits. You dreamed big dreams. There were no doubts planted. No one had told you to grow up and be realistic. No one had defined who you were and who you were not. Nothing was wrong with you. You belonged nowhere and everywhere.

Looking back to Chapter Eight, what were some of your superpowers you listed? Are you using those in your life currently? How could you translate these superpowers so you could contribute to the world? Have you ever thought about what you want your legacy to be?

These are big questions. After letting go of your limitations and limiting beliefs in the previous chapters, I invite you to start to look at what more could be possible for your life.

Take a few minutes and start to explore these questions. How could you use what is great about you to make life better for yourself and others? What would you want to leave as your legacy?____

____

____

____

Someone I respect greatly, the co-founder of Norwex, Debbie Bolton, shared with me that one year she chose her word of the year to be '*more*.' I love that! If there were ever a word that summed up the experience of thriving in the world, it would be 'more.' That word shouts possibility and no limits! You have gone from looking at the ways you have limited and been surviving life to opening yourself to the idea of thriving. Now it is time to take one hundred percent responsibility for being the creator in what your life looks like. Let us look at how to create that '*more*' for you!

Before I ask what you want, let us look at what can stop us; it is an ugly four-letter word that starts with '*F*!' Fear!

Fear is a thought. It is an energy we hold onto. It is an experience that we accumulate in our bodies. We make it significant then hoard and store it in our bodies and we live like it is happening. We go out of our way to prove to ourselves that the world is not a safe place. Then we let the physical experiences and reactions of fear that we have hoarded in our bodies validate that there is indeed something to worry about in our world. The thing is, this is completely irrational.

What we are fearing is not really happening at the moment. I am afraid that I will fail. I am afraid of being made fun of. I am afraid I might not have enough money. I am afraid of getting my heart broken. And when I have these thoughts, based on past experiences, there is a physical reaction that happens in my body. That physical response confirms for me that there must be something legitimately to fear. But there is nothing to fear at the moment. What is happening is my worry about the future and/or my body remembering what it felt like when it happened in the past. What is happening is I am having a thought and a body sensation that mirrors that thought.

Fear is irrational when there is nothing to fear. When we are reacting to *thoughts* about a *potential* future but it is not what is actually happening at the moment, it is unfounded to be afraid. Consider this definition of fear: False Evidence Appearing Real.

So what do we do about this experience of fear and how it feels so real? Learn to allow it and recognize that it is a feeling brought on by your thoughts. Trust that you are safe. Notice what is happening is an experience *within* you, not an experience outside of you. Allow the fear to move through you like a river flowing out to sea. Release and choose trust.

Choose trust, not just in the world, but trust in yourself to handle whatever happens. See that the experience of fear is there to help you break through challenges and boundaries. You experience fear in a situation because that situation, relationship or outcome is important to you and new to you. When you experience fear it simply means that you do not have enough growth and confidence in that particular area of your life. Yet.

Instead of fear, be grateful to yourself for stepping into something that is a stretch for you. Be grateful for all the good that there is now. Be grateful for the challenges that are in service to your future self. Fear is part of the process, and it is normal. Just do not hang out in fear for too long. You do not want to buy into the fear and have it dictate how you show up.

Notice the habitual place and actions that you go to when you start to experience fear. Do you drink? Feel tired? Numb out with busy or work? Shut down? Eat? There is tremendous power in the ability to catch yourself and to be able to observe your instinctive responses and behaviours to fear. See these experiences as a reaction you have, not a confirmation of what is real.

When you do see these fears, meet yourself with absolute compassion and love. Remember, we are not here to fight the old ways of being but to build upon new ones. Nothing is wrong with how you feel. It just becomes a question of workability and whether how you feel serves what you want for your life.

I heard a great quote once, “It is always scary until it is not!” The only way it is not going to be scary is if you choose to push through in those moments when you feel like you cannot or when it feels uncomfortable. Just take the next *right* step. And then the next one. And then the next. And remember that as you step into your greatness, that feeling '*ready*' is a lie! We acquire feeling '*ready*' and the confidence we desire from having done something before. Just as we acquire wisdom from personal trials and learning, we become '*ready*' by taking actions before we feel '*ready*' to take them. Feel the fear and do it anyway.

In moments when you feel the pressure in your body, and you are certain that the fear is real, try saying, "Wow, this is really stretching me." Use the power of your language. You become '*ready*' when you choose not to give in to fear and instead create the mindset of being grateful that the fear is present. You tell yourself, "I am thrilled that I am feeling a bit fearful because it means I am growing and stretching." Remember, something only needs to be fifty percent believable and said with emotion for the mind to run with it.

We can choose to be brave before we feel ready. Let me say it again; we can choose to be brave before we feel ready. Which is not the absence of fear but rather the willingness to feel the fear and move forward anyway. Fear is an energy. When we become aware of this, we can see it for what it is and allow it to move through us. In acknowledging and giving fear our attention, it loses its power over us. It is much like shame. When we speak the unspeakable, it loses the power to exist in our minds as the truth. It stops living within us.

Until now, the invisible force of fear has been your constant companion. It has influenced every decision and directed every choice and relationship. It has appeared at pivotal moments to steer you away from stepping powerfully into your greatness and into who you are created to be. It is the voice in your head telling you no, you cannot do it or it is dangerous to try. It is the sound of defeat. Fear steals your joy, fulfillment and experience of life.

Something fun to try taking on fear is to make a '*Fear List.*' What are the greatest fears that hold you back? Make a list of all the things you fear and circle the top three. _______________

____

____

____

Set a thirty, sixty and ninety-day challenge of taking the next *right* step despite your fear. Really take it on. Your authentic power will come from the confidence that grows in doing this. You cannot outthink your fears. You cannot journal them out. You must take bold action to move past them. Go all in on your fears until they disappear. The next level for your life lives on the other side of the things you fear the most!

I wrote this book the year I chose '*brave*' as my word of the year. So, many times, fear would overtake my ability to show up and write. My stomach would be in knots, my heart would race, and my mind would go blank. Sometimes I would feel too exhausted to focus. Sometimes I felt nauseous. This was fear manifesting itself physically. I would start asking myself, why am I even writing this? Who will it make a difference for? Why am I wasting my time and neglecting all the other things in my life? I had to choose to be brave and tell myself nothing dangerous was actually happening. I had to breathe through the physical symptoms and show up regardless of how I felt. We forget how powerful the breath is, especially in moving tough emotions along. Sometimes we just need to breathe.

The challenge with choosing to be brave was it opened me up to so much vulnerability. I would literally get vulnerability hangovers, sometimes for days after I chose to be brave in a situation. It would sometimes even have me retreat and pull back. That openness and vulnerability felt so uncomfortable that I was certain it was a sign that I was headed in the wrong direction.

Like the physical sensations of fear felt real, so too do the physical reactions to being vulnerable. Each time I was '*taken out'* by stepping out of my comfort zone, I would have to rebuild myself to show up again. Continuously recovering and showing up, strengthened my ability to be brave. And as my ability to be brave strengthened, I got taken out less and recovered faster.

Soon, a deeper strength and gratitude started to open up in my life. It was like my capacity for life grew. I saw the blessings and possibilities in a new way. It was as if I had started to excavate fear from the garden of my life. Instead of pulling the weeds, I had brought in an excavator, and now I was digging deep. New space was now available.

When we allow ourselves to be vulnerable, we experience a blessing. Our confidence and trust expands. We are offering ourselves the opportunity to see and experience life authentically. Ironically, the certainty we cling to in order to feel safe in life comes from stepping outside of our certainty and that requires being brave and vulnerable. It can be developed with simple two millimetre shifts in your mindset. By being brave and choosing empowered thinking, you develop confidence and certainty. Then with that confidence, you begin to see that you can create a life you love that fulfills you. Just as Glinda the good witch tells Dorothy in the Wizard of Oz, you have always had the power within.

Fear has tried to serve you. It tried to do its job. It tried to keep you safe and alive, yet fear has also limited your life. It is time to take back your power. Like a friend you have outgrown and with whom you must now part ways, it is time to say, "thank you fear but you no longer serve my goals and dreams." It is time to move on into a healthy relationship with fear. One where you control the emotion and accept fear with gratitude for the opportunity for growth that it is bringing you.

It is time to step into a greater life, a greater experience and a greater truth. It is time to step into the greatest you!

The world needs you to be great and to share the contributions that you have to bring! Did you know that there is no one else with your identical fingerprint, eye pigmentation, vocal timbre, gait, or ways of seeing the world? Therefore, no one else can feel, see, walk or speak the truth that is unique to you. There is no one else in the world who can bring what you can bring.

Your joy, fulfillment and power lie in embracing what makes you different and expressing the wholeness of your true self!

You know those people who are lovely to be around? Who have a sense of grace, peace and purpose so much so that you wonder if they ever went through anything difficult. They are themselves. And as we become more ourselves, we are also more becoming to others. We spend so much time comparing ourselves to others and trying to fit in before we realize we do not nor are we supposed to fit in; we are all created unique.

Consider that you were made to stand out! Consider that you have unique gifts to bring to the world and that playing small and pretending you are not special serves no one. People will miss out on what you can offer if you hide yourself. Think about who loses when you do not win!

The fear of stepping into what is uniquely great about you is way less uncomfortable than the life you miss out on when you do not go for it. Discomfort is inevitable. Fear is inevitable. You can stay small, secure and safe but ultimately, that will cost you your life's potential and purpose. And let me tell you, that gets really uncomfortable and sad.

Have you ever heard the saying that comparison is the thief of joy? Never compare yourself!

You can reference other people to see what is possible but do not dare compare! Comparing yourself to others lets you off the hook for stepping into how great you are. Let go of trying to get or be more of what you do not need or what your weaknesses are. Pay attention to your strengths and what you already have, and it will expand.

What you appreciate, appreciates!

When you commit to making a difference with what you already have and what you are already capable of, it expands. Especially when you share it with others. Making a difference in your life makes a difference in other people's lives. Never play small or pretend that you are anything less than the amazing self you are!

Do not mask yourself as a horse when you know in your heart that you are a unicorn!

"The meaning of life is to find your gift. The purpose of life is to give it away."

~Pablo Picasso

I want you to think of when you are your happiest, most fulfilled and confident self. Think of the love and joy you spread. The kindness, the wise words, the connections. How do you treat your partner?____

____

What about your kids?____________________________

____

Your friends and family?____________________________

____

What are the experiences they are having because of you?_

____

What is that sense of pride you feel? Is it the knowledge that this is who you are and what you can bring to your people and the world?

Now think of when you are feeling underappreciated, stressed, overwhelmed—when you have that sense that nothing you do is good enough. That you are on your own and everything is on your shoulders. That no one sees you, gets you or cares—when you feel like you might explode into tears or screams or both! When you are filled with resentment, anger, guilt, hurt and shame. Who are you to your partner? How do you talk to them?

____

____

What about the kids? What are your interactions like with them?____

____

Do you make time for connections with family and friends? If you do, how do you feel about how you leave them feeling from your interaction?__________________________________

____

What is that feeling at the end of the day about what you have put out into the world?______________________________

____

Who is losing because you are not creating a life in which you win? Do you get it yet?

You have to own your greatness! You must do everything possible to be your best self! And you are worth whatever amount of time that it takes!

You say you do not have the time for you? Bullshit! We make time for what is important. Instead of saying, "I do not have time," try saying, "I am not a priority," and see how that feels."I am not a priority." It is even hard to write that sentence. It feels so wrong. Other things are hard too. Try saying, "I am not going to submit your resume sweetie, because what is important to you is not a priority." "I do not go to the doctor because my health is not a priority." If these phrases do not sit well, that is the point.

Changing our language reminds us that time, like our mindset, is a choice. It is our choice to make ourselves a priority. And it is okay if this has not been your choice. Maybe you did not know until now how extremely essential and important making time for your self-care and development is.

"Do the best you can until you know better. Then when you know better, do better.

~ Maya Angelou

One of the main excuses I hear from busy moms is how they cannot do certain things or do not have the time they need because of their kids. Use your kids as your reason to make yourself a priority, not as your excuse to neglect yourself. The best thing you can do for your kids is to take great care of their mother. What do you want their future lives to be like? What kind of relationship do you want them to have with themselves as adults and mothers? Then it is essential that you get yourself together and make yourself a priority.

You cannot tell your kids who and how to be; you have to show them.

And it is the same for your relationship. The best thing you can do for your partner is to love and care for yourself. Your people need you to be well. The world needs you to be well. If not for you, do it for them! And don't you dare act like a martyr; playing all poor me and choosing to sacrifice so much, then blaming your people for your choices!

I say this because seeing and living into your greatness is my absolute mission in life! You being free from limitations, living into your greatness and impacting the world drives me to be brave. My greatest wish for you is to come to know and be the extraordinary Self you already are. That you live your extraordinary Self in each moment of your life, from this day forward. I am inviting you to rise up. I am standing up for your life! Will you stand for it with me?

"When a woman rises up in her glory, her energy is magnetic and her sense of possibility is contagious"
~ Marianne Williamson

CHAPTER FOURTEEN

Life's Purpose Fulfilled

"Do not wait for everything to be perfect before you decide to enjoy your life."

Let us start to dream again. If you knew you could not fail, what would you take on? If no was not an option, what would you try? If you were living your story, not the one told that you should be living, what would you be doing? Who would you get busy being? What would you stand for? Play the game. Go big! Les Brown says your dreams should scare you! What experience would cause our old friend *'fear'* to appear? Really go for it here! There are no right or wrong answers. It is not about what your circumstances are. Give this space to your heart to express what is there beneath all the *'shoulds' 'cants' 'yeah buts' 'what ifs.'* Give yourself time to explore. It may be buried deep inside you.

It may help to open things up if you write with your non-dominant hand while you ask yourself, "If anything is possible, what would I want for my life?"________________________

____

____

____

Do not stop there. Ask yourself, "If anything were possible, who would I want to be? What would the most authentic, open, honouring, and fully expressed version of myself be?"________

____

____

____

How much fun was that?

I will be honest. It takes me some time to really get free to dream. Sometimes I think I am too cerebral or rational. I found that as soon as I get really into it, I skip over to the thought of '*yeah, but how*?'

Dreaming is not about *how*. It is about allowing yourself to indulge in fantasizing about something you greatly desire. It is a form of play. It is an invitation to go back to when we were children, free to be, to express and to play. There were no limits on what was possible. If that time in your life feels too far away or like freedom was never your childhood way of being, I invite you to spend time around kids six or younger. Watch how they play. Watch how they are free to be in life. That experience is available to you too. If you look, that sense of play is still there. It does not go away with age.

As we allow ourselves the freedom to play and to dream, we want to ground those dreams in our current lives. Ask yourself, who would I have to be to have this in my life? What do people who have what I dream about think or do? What do they feel and believe? You may have heard the phrase, dress for the job you want. This is like that. Live like you have the life you want.

Write down a few ideas about who you would have to be for these dreams to exist in your life. Is it a one-word quality like my being '*brave*?' Maybe it is a description of a way you would look or show up. There are no right or wrong answers. Look at it like who is your ideal self, and then go even further. Have fun dreaming about what is possible for who you can be when you are being your best self.______________________________

____

____

____

No matter how long you have headed in a direction away from your true Self, you always have the choice to change course. It is what it is. You are where you are. You did what you did, and you did not do what you did not do. Accept it, learn from it and choose to grow from it. Where you are is not who you are unless you choose to keep being that person. Your past does not determine your future unless you unpack and decide to stay there.

Most days, I wake up and I have to remind myself, there is nothing wrong here. There is nothing wrong with me. I have patterns to unlearn, new behaviours to embody and wounds to heal. But there is nothing *wrong with the core of me and who I am.* I am unlearning generations of harm and letting go, embracing love and being brave. It takes time. The tough thing is that in the past, I have not been great at being a patient person!

I remember another key thing my Landmark coach Sheryl Pearson said to me, " Brandy, there is no top to this mountain. We are not here to fix you or to change you because you are not broken, and nothing is wrong." I remember thinking, well shit! Why am I paying for this course then?! I was certain that something was wrong with me and that they would have the answer to what would help me arrive at the life I was meant to live. After I got over being peeved at her words, I got the freedom that came with them.

What if there was nowhere to get to? What if I could create the game of enjoying the journey all the time? What if it was not about fixing my broken self but standing in my greatness and creating a life I loved? What if nothing was wrong and *everything was possible*?!?!

What if you are not broken either? What if you can begin *right now* enjoying your life and loving where you are while still growing and stretching to the *'something more'* within you?!

Have you considered that you could have a lot of fun creating a new identity for yourself? You can be anything! What is your desired outcome? What will you put behind the words '*I am*?' You decide who you are and what you are here for! You declare who you are for the world!

Every morning, when I wake up, I like to start my day by creating myself as a possibility. Who I am today, as I write this, is the possibility of resilience and contribution. Who I was yesterday was the possibility of strength and power.

Who do you say you are as a possibility today? Who I am is the possibility of____

____

____

____

You are the greatest project you will ever get to work on. Take your time. Create absolute magic.

Remember when I said, what is wrong is available but so is what is right? That applies to you. What is right and great about you is available at this very moment without any single thing altering. Focus on your strengths. A lot of time we spend energy trying to transform areas where we are not strong and neglect to see, appreciate and develop what we are already good at.

Stop shaming yourself for what you did not know then and start improving yourself with what you know now. You do not have to be good at everything. Remember, where your focus goes, energy will flow. Focus your energy on what is great about you!

What are some of your strengths and gifts? Don't be shy! Own them! ____

____

____

____

"If you can't love yourself, how in the hell you gonna love somebody else?" ~RuPaul

Another key way to step into your life's purpose and your greatness is to reframe your limitations. In doing this, you let go of what you may have told yourself was not good enough or wrong about you. Instead, you show yourself that you are on your side and all parts of you are a gift. You become whole.

Often, I was teased and criticized for being a talker and always taking center stage. Well, here is that talker now writing a book and speaking greatness into people! All parts of me are a gift! My disorganization at work allows me a lot of space to be creative! The way I always have to make everyone a friend has given me a lot of great friendships!

Everything can be a positive if you choose to see it that way. Reframe your limitations.

What is something you often see or have been told is a detriment? ______________________________

____

____

____

How can you reframe that into a positive or blessing? What positives have these ways of being gotten you? ____________

____

____

____

Lastly, take a look at how you can keep this new identity alive. Share it with others, not all others, only the ones who you can trust to hold your dreams. My friend and the Co-Founder of Norwex, Debbie Bolton, wisely advised me, "Watch who you share your dreams with as not everyone can carry them. God gave them to you, not them."

Build a structure for your dreams. Make a plan. Some ideas for structure are; reminders in your phone, a vision board, goal tracking, sticky notes, playlist in your phone, hire someone who can help you, and make a promise to yourself.

What else can you think of that will work to remind you of what you are working towards?______________________________

____

____

____

Remember, the default conversation that exists in life and out in the world is what is wrong. If you are going to stand for what is right and what you want, you need to keep it constantly in front of you, so you do not slide into the default conversation and wake up one day saying, "How the heck did I get here?"

Always watch how you speak about yourself. I want to remind you that you hear yourself talk. Listen. Be responsible for your language. Ask yourself, "Is this kind of talk going to empower and uplift me, or am I being mean, disempowering and playing small?" Hold on to the idea of talking to yourself like you would to a small child or best friend. Be your own best friend!

And remember, you are not always a certain way. There is nothing you '*should*,' '*need*' or '*have*' to do. It is not funny to be the brunt of jokes. You shrinking so that others do not feel intimidated around you serves no one, especially you!

"There will always be someone who can't see your worth. Don't let it be you! ~Mel Robbins

Even more important than watching your language is watching your mindset. Like you feed your body daily, intentionally feed your mind daily as well. I love starting my day with Tony Robbins' Priming exercise to put my mindset in a powerful place of gratitude, love and vision. I also listen to podcasts or YouTube videos as I get ready in the morning. I keep a playlist of favourites and inspirations. Music really helps alter my mindset, so I have different playlists depending on what experience I need to create for myself.

Develop a system to deactivate any negative thoughts that come, as they will still come. First, notice the negative thought and how it makes you feel. Then, forgive yourself for having that thought and then reach for the next best feeling or thought available to you. To help you do this, keep a list or journal of affirmations or empowering thoughts handy. Build a toolbox for yourself to be able to live in an intentionally joyful and empowered state. It does not happen by chance or luck. However, it does get easier as you strengthen the muscle of a positive mindset. It starts with deciding to be happy for no reason!

Accept compliments. Let people fill your cup and contribute to you. Our openness to receiving is paramount to our abundance in life. People or the universe cannot give you anything unless you are open to receiving it. Not being open to receiving it is based on your feelings of self-worth.

Ask yourself these five questions to show if you are open to receiving the good from others or if you push it away.

1. Do you have a hard time accepting a compliment, or do you take it in?
2. Do you have a hard time receiving gifts?
3. Do you have a hard time asking for or receiving help and support?
4. Do you have a hard time accepting things that come easily?
5. Do you downplay what is good in your life because you do not want others to feel bad?

Do not judge yourself if it becomes clear that you have a hard time receiving the good. This is just a starting point from which to measure your progress.

Take a deep breath, put your hand on your heart and ask yourself, how can I open myself up to receiving, right now, in this moment?____

____

____

____

Ask yourself, what is the most loving thing I can do for myself right now?____

Then go do it! It does not matter what you do; it matters that you are paying attention to yourself. Do it for more than you! Be the light that helps others see. By standing in your greatness and allowing yourself to shine, you liberate others to do the same.

"You cannot get through a single day without having an impact on the world around you. What you do makes a difference.

And you have to decide what kind of difference you want to make." ~Jane Goodall

Let go of the belief that everything has to be done by you. To all my mothers out there: Do not be a martyr! Leverage your time. Dump everything you do onto a piece of paper and then ask, what can I eliminate, delegate and automate? Teach your kids how to help and show them the benefits to their life when mommy is happy and at peace. My youngest knows that the biggest consequence of her not cleaning up is that mommy then has to do it, and we will not have time together to play. You want to grow valuable humans who know they are able, capable and powerful! Do not make your children's lives so easy that you cripple them.

Remember that all human progress is preceded by a new question. The quality of those questions determines the quality of our lives. A question like, "why do these things always happen to me?" versus "how can I make this a blessing?" will create two totally different experiences and lives.

To change your life, change your questions.

Embrace gratitude! Embrace self-appreciation and embrace the magical moments that are constant. Remember, where focus goes, energy flows. Starting and ending your day with a Gratitude and Self-Appreciation Journal can be so powerful. You will look for the things in your day to later write about. It will have you focus on finding things you love and are grateful for in the world and yourself!

What we appreciate, appreciates!

Gratitude brings more of what we love into our lives. I once heard someone say, everyday I write ten things that I am grateful for, and on hard days, I write one hundred! Another great tip is to keep a journal app on your phone titled '*Magical Moments*.' As you go about your day, set a goal to capture five magical moments throughout your day. Again, this helps shape your focus and will alter the experience of your day!

Ultimately, stay connected to yourself! Set a time for heart-centred time with yourself. Create it into existence by developing a system and schedule for it. Take time to sit quietly with your hand on your heart, breathing in love, peace, compassion and joy.

Self-care can be so simple. What matters is that it is done purposefully and consistently.

"If there is light in the soul, there will be beauty in the person.
If there is beauty in the person, there will be harmony in the house.
If there is harmony in the house, there will be order in the nation.
If there is order in the nation, there will be peace in the world. ~Chinese proverb

CHAPTER FIFTEEN

Bringing Your Dreams Alive

"You don't have to see the whole staircase. Just take the first step."

~Martin Luther King Jr.

This chapter is about where the proverbial "rubber meets the road." It is great to feel inspired, to see something new and to declare a new possibility. But that makes no real difference unless you take action upon this new possibility.

I have said a few times throughout this book that you can have your reasons or your results. Have you dug down deep yet and decided which one you will accept and stand for from now on?

Choosing results means giving up playing small and pretending that you are anything less than extraordinary. It means letting go of your stories, your certainties, and your reasons and excuses for why you cannot bring out the best version of yourself. The voice in your head that says you cannot do this is a liar! You are so much more than your circumstances and past!

"It is hard to breathe life into a dream when you're choking on excuses!" ~ Billy Alsbrooks

Before we talk about actions to take, it is important for me to say this — you can do anything, but you cannot do everything. Really hear that. You can do *anything,* but you cannot do *everything*!

I have been so guilty of trying to do too much and then not doing anything to the best of my ability. The worst part of this experience is when you feel like you are doing your best and going as hard as you can, but still, it never feels good enough. Who can relate to that? Well, no more of that, I say!

Without a clear plan, what will steal your attention are three things:

1. Anything you think will lead to pain
2. Things you think will lead to immediate pleasure
3. Other people's demands (which as a mom are many)

When developing your plan, you need to be specific. Focus on progress, getting a little better consistently, not on perfection. The secret to your success is simpler than you might think. You can find it in your daily routine. You change your life when you change something you do daily. Nothing huge. One *right* step at a time. Master that new habit and then move on to another.

"If you cannot do great things, do small things in a great way." ~Napolean Hill

Make sure to account for '*lag time.*' The delay between action and results. When I am taking on a new habit or way of being, I have to constantly remind myself that I did not become the current me overnight. Sometimes I can be so impatient when I want to create a new result or make a change— compassion and grace with yourself are key. I believe we are always doing our best in a given moment. It may not be the best that we want, but given where we are at, what we are handling, it is the best we have to give at the moment.

Progress only happens when you become conscious of what you want.

Ask yourself three questions:

1. What do I want?______________________________

____

____

____

2. Why do I want it?_____________________________

____

____

____

3. How am I going to get it?______________________

____

____

____

The worst question to ask yourself is, what *should* I *do?* We human beings are constantly focused on the doing. The life we live is so much more than that. It is based on who we are being, where we are headed and what difference we can make. We are human beings, not human doings!

Focus on what you want, not on what you do not want. If I ask people what they want, most will tell me all the things they do not want. That is easy. We need to refocus the brain on what we *do want*. Remember, where focus goes, energy flows. Do you want your energy to flow to what you do not want or on what you do want?

Before we go any further with what to focus on, I also want you to make a list of what not to focus on. A *'stop doing'* list. This is a powerful idea that Dean Graziosi teaches. What are one or two things that you focus on that do not serve you? Remember, we have to be aware of our thoughts before we can change them. So, what do you focus on that makes you feel worried, stressed or anxious? What is something that you do regularly that you do not have to do? Be honest with yourself. ____________________

____

____

____

I would be so busy all the time that I felt like a total victim to my schedule. When I got honest about why I was so busy, it became clear that I was subconsciously trying to prove to others that I was valuable. It was exhausting, and I felt like I had no freedom or power. I had to choose to stop valuing '*busy*.' I will not even allow the word to come out of my mouth anymore.

Language creates our world. Once I understood that, I became intentional in letting go of the value I had placed on '*busy*.' I also became conscious of not buying into what others would say about my life. I get that the common way to describe how we do life is '*busy,*' but I refuse to take on that description. I choose the stuff that goes in my daytimer. I choose the level of how I parent. I choose the expectations I have for myself. I choose the projects, the commitments and the goals. My life is not happening *to me*, so I refuse for it to be described as though it is. When people say, "Wow, you are so busy!" I answer, "Yes, it is an abundant life of things that I chose to say yes to and that I love."

Do not defend or try to change how others view your life. It does not matter what others think of your life; it matters what you think! How you respond helps to teach the language and energy that you want people to use to describe your life. You teach people how to treat you.

"We seldom realize, for example, our most private thoughts and emotions are not actually our own. We think in terms of languages and images which we did not invent, but which were given to us by our society" ~ Alan Watts

It is important to try not to fall into assuming ill intent from people. Maybe what you are certain is criticism is actually the person communicating something else. Try to listen beyond their words. When people call me 'busy', I sometimes hear that they are trying to tell me they need some of my time and attention or are feeling neglected. Often people do not have the awareness or skills to always communicate what they really need.

I hope all the chapters up till now have inspired you. I anticipate that you have taken a lot away—concepts, new ways of thinking and seeing the world, a sense of freedom and qualities that did not exist before. All of these are great new ideas, but unless they are followed with powerful, intentional action, they are empty. Now that you have gained awareness about yourself and your life, you want to decide where to focus your energies. When you decide where to look, know that whatever you are not changing, you are choosing. Said another way, what you permit, you promote.

I have the privilege of watching my six-year-old daughter play with her friends. They create the most elaborate creative games with everything that they do. Even playing Barbies has a game theme. I will hear her say, "Okay, so we are roommates, and you are going to school." They structure their play as if it is a game of life. When did we lose that imagination and sense of play with our life? We can choose to do that with our lives every day. We can structure our lives with play. We can choose to make it all a game. And you get to decide what your game looks and feels like. You decide what winning looks like to you and what is worth winning. If you are in your own game, there is no such thing as a wrong move. And please play full out in your game! Play to win as opposed to playing not to lose.

And do not play the game in the future. Play the game right now, as now is the time that is currently happening. The future does not exist. Play daily! If you find yourself frustrated, depressed or stressed, you are often playing someone else's game. You have stopped playing your game, created by you, for you. Play *your game*!

What do you say matters in your game of life?____________

____

____

____

As I said before, a key process I engage in for everything I take on is to set an intention. In my relationships, my interactions, the jobs I am doing, in everything. I set an intention for what I want the outcome to be before I go into the situation. It helps me be more aware and conscious of what I am bringing to the table, who I am being and what my actions are so that I am more likely to get my desired outcome. If left to my default human way of being, I can sometimes miss opportunities to get the most out of experiences and my relationships.

The intention you have informs the action you take. This is where you want to start. Always look at what your honest intention is so you can understand your actions better.

I used to have the disease to please. I would get so upset when people did not acknowledge me for what I had contributed. When I started to look at why I was so triggered, I could see that it was because my intention was to please and to get somewhere with them. So when I would not get their acknowledgement, I had '*failed'* in my mind.

To know what actions to start with, ask yourself, "What would make the biggest difference in my life right now?" Or said another way, "What can I focus on that will make everything else in my life work better?" Brainstorm a few ideas of the next right step for your life.______________________________

____

____

____

Focus on one to three things maximum that you want to master in your life. Once you feel like they have become a habit or are mastered, then choose another one. That is how you build a life that you love. You do not have to do it all overnight. Lots of little right actions focused on a powerful intention lead you to your life of greatness.

Remember, it is always going to feel scary until it is not. '*Ready'* is a lie. We never feel ready. The only way it is not going to be scary is when you push forward, even when you get scared or uncomfortable. Get comfortable being uncomfortable.

What we focus on grows.

In moving forward, there are six steps to focus on:

Step 1. Pay attention to your energy. Get in your happy place. Make sure that you are a vibrational match to what you want to attract in your life. Your life is not happening to you. It is reflecting you.

Step 2. Set an intention. Recite it to yourself as you look in your eyes in the mirror every morning. Add the emotion and stand in the present as if what you want or who you want to be already is.

Step 3. Get clear about what you want. Watch your language! State what you want in the present. State it positively. Talk about what you do want, not what you do not want.

Step 4. Visualize your life. Put yourself in the scene of your own life. Use all your senses and get specific. What am I seeing, feeling, doing and smelling in this new time in my life? This creates new neural pathways in your brain. Think of it as daydreaming with intention.

Step 5. Take the next right step. You must take action to get where you want to go. Everything matters and is a breadcrumb that will lead you to something else. Take the next right step!

Step 6. Surrender to the belief that everything that is happening is for your highest good. Trust. Stand in the space that life is happening for you, not to you and look for the lessons and blessings.

Next, watch who you give a seat at the table to. Have you heard proximity is power? You become like the five people that you most hang out with.

I believe that and have seen it for my own life. Choosing people that fit my future and not my past has been so powerful in keeping me encouraged, motivated and connected to the direction I am going. That being said, it does not mean to cancel out and write off everyone from your past. That is for you to decide who you will bring forward in your life. One of the best ways I have heard of handling this transition is in Jamie Kern Lima's book "*Believe It*!" She talks about looking at who we give the microphone in our lives to, how long we give it to them and how loud we turn the volume up. I love this because sometimes people will say you need to move on from people and I do not feel that is always a viable or necessary solution.

As I mentioned before, one of my key mentors in my life, Debbie Bolton, tells me, "Be careful who you share your dreams with because not everybody is capable of holding them." I believe that sometimes what people say to us about our lives and our dreams says more about them than it does about us. It shows their capabilities to dream big and how much they trust.

I have no doubt that my mother loves me and wants the best for me. Oftentimes she will be the one to say '*what if*' and '*Are you sure that is what you want to do*?' She will default to what she thinks is a safe choice for me. I know that is out of her love for me and desire to keep me safe or make sure that I do not get hurt. I do not need to hate her, be angry about it or decide that she does not *get* me. Yet, I also do not always need to take her advice. And in the space of taking a hundred percent responsibility for my life, I author my life.

My mother instinctively still tries to protect me. Growing up with depression, suicidal tendencies, being sexually assaulted multiple times, having an eating disorder and low self-esteem, I cannot imagine how painful it was for my mother to watch me suffer. Not to mention the drama that I expressed my confusion and pain through.

I cannot complete this book without recognizing and acknowledging the phenomenal job both of my parents did in simply keeping me alive. But they did more than that; they gave me a solid foundation to always return to. They gave me unconditional love and strength when I could not even recognize it for myself. No matter how messy I got, they never gave up on me, nor did my best friend Sylvia or my sister Michelle. They truly are the wind beneath my wings, and they all held the vision of a greater, happier me when I could not see it. And although I do not always love it, they do not let me play small or stay in my pity party for too long. They challenge me in a loving way. Know that the person who challenges you and holds you accountable is more beneficial to your life than the person who watches you stay the same and settle for mediocrity.

Ultimately, it is about loving yourself enough to surround yourself with people who respect you. The company you keep is a reflection of how you feel about yourself.

"When you learn how much you are worth, you will stop giving people discounts."

You are not required to set yourself on fire to keep other people warm. Once you learn how to be truly happy, you will not tolerate being around people who make you feel anything less. You will get that your value does not decrease based on someone's inability to see your worth.

And as for you, be a woman other women can trust. Have the courage to tell another woman directly when she offends, hurts or disappoints you. Be a woman who lifts other women.

"Your new life is going to cost you your old one. It is going to cost you your comfort zone and your sense of direction. It's going to cost you some relationships and friends. It's going to cost you being liked and understood. But it doesn't matter. Because the people who are meant for you are going to meet you on the other side. And you are going to build a new comfort zone around the things that actually move you forward. And instead of being liked, you were going to be loved. Instead of understanding, you are going to be seen. All you're going to lose is what was built for the person you no longer are. Let It Go." ~Brianna Wiest

CHAPTER SIXTEEN

It Starts with Self

"We but mirror the world. All the tendencies present in the outer world are to be found in the world of our body. If we could change ourselves, the tendencies in the world would also change. As a man changes his own nature, so does the attitude of the world change towards him. This is the divine mystery supreme. A wonderful thing it is and the source of our happiness. We need not wait to see what others do."
~Mahatma Gandhi

One of the coolest things I heard about how to show up in your own life was: If you imagined your life as a story, would you be the heroine you would cheer for?

Often, especially as women and mothers, we tend to be super hard on ourselves. It cannot only be me. In this space as a mother, it is so easy to focus on what is wrong or where we believe we are not enough. Remember that while you are busy doubting yourself, someone else is admiring your strength. Your basement floor is someone else's top floor.

We will have moments of breakdown. Moments where we forget, hopefully only for a brief time, how extraordinary we are. You are human. It is okay to have a meltdown. Just do not unpack and live there. Cry it out. Call a friend. Blast the tunes. Then refocus on the amazing life that you are committed to creating.

Be patient when becoming someone you have not allowed yourself to be before. You did not become this current version of yourself overnight either. Just because you are struggling does not mean you are failing.

When a child is learning to walk and falls down fifty times, they never think to themselves, "maybe this isn't for me."

Be thankful for what you are now, and keep standing for what you want to be tomorrow. Bring self-love and gratitude to yourself in this present moment. Do not wait to hit your goals before you celebrate yourself. There is so much to celebrate along the way!

One of the best words that I took on for myself through this journey of growth, was grace. As a high achiever and multi-passionate person, I would often get caught up in producing end results. I had become a human doing, not a human being. Not only was I addicted to producing results, but I also had my whole sense of self-worth tied into it. I was good if I achieved, and I was bad if I did not. Even my downtime had to have a purpose to it. As you can imagine or maybe relate to, it was exhausting! There was always so much pressure. And I got tired of people telling me, "You are so hard on yourself!" It was not like they were telling me something I did not already know. I just did not know how to stop it. It was like being on a roller coaster that felt out of control. All I could do was go along for the ride until I decided to stop it and get off.

When I committed to bringing grace into my life, the pressure and anxiety I felt eased. Windows of joy in my daily life started to let light in. I saw a richness in my days that was not there before. Gradually, it became easier to lay my head on the pillow at night, knowing that no matter what I had or had not achieved, I could allow grace. I slept more soundly. Like everything else, grace was a choice. I had to be kind and willing to bring love, compassion and acceptance to myself. I had to *give* myself grace.

"You can't hate yourself happy. You can't criticize yourself thin. You can't shame yourself worthy. Real change begins with self-love and self-care." ~Jessica Ortner

Growth is uncomfortable because you have never been here before. You have never been this version of you. So give yourself a little grace and stay true to your commitment to yourself.

After grace came self-acceptance, self-love, self-honouring and self-care. It was a lot of self. The thing is, there is a difference between self and selfish. My commitment to self was to develop myself to be the best version for people around me.

I recognize for some of you, focusing on yourself may seem selfish, or you may not even know where to begin. Self-love is asking yourself what you need every single day and then making sure you receive it. It is treating yourself the way you would treat a small child. Feed yourself healthy food. Make sure you spend some time outside. Put yourself to bed early and let yourself take naps. Do not say mean things to yourself and do not put yourself in danger with situations or people.

To help you focus and develop self-love, there are a few questions that you can ask yourself.

Will this action move me towards the future and life I want, or will it keep me stuck in my patterns of the past?

Will this choice bring me long-term fulfillment or short-term satisfaction?

Am I standing in my power right now, or am I trying to please someone else?

Am I looking for what is right, or am I looking for what is wrong?

Am I holding onto my reasons, or am I focused on my results?

Does this action empower or disempower me?

Am I acting from faith or from fear?

Am I using my voice in its full expression and standing in my truth, or am I shrinking, so others do not feel uncomfortable?

Will I use this situation or outcome to learn and grow or am I choosing to beat myself up and feel bad?

Am I falling into emotional patterns and the comfort of my emotional house, or am I choosing love, resilience, compassion and grace?

"We are not held back by the love we didn't receive in the past, but by the love we are not extending in the present." ~Marianne Williamson

With every act of self-care, your authentic self gets stronger, and the critical, fearful mind gets weaker. Every act of self-care is a powerful declaration that *I am on my side*, and I have got my own back.

Remember back in the beginning when I said that what hurts us the most is the ways that we abuse, abandon, mistreat and neglect ourselves? When I am not true to myself, I abandon myself. When I step into my commitment for self-love and self-care, I am rebuilding trust and a relationship with *the one who matters the most—me*!

"We can't ask people to give us something that we do not believe we are worthy of receiving. And you will know you're worthy of receiving it when you trust yourself above everyone else." ~Brene Brown

When we honour who we are, our self-esteem grows. When we stand in the space of self-acceptance, we are free from the burden of needing anyone else to accept us. We get that it is not other people's jobs to like us. It is ours!

When self-love is present in your relationships with people, it does not mean that everyone will treat you the way you think you deserve to be treated. It means that you will not let them change the way you see yourself, nor will you stick around for them to hurt you.

If you do not see your worth, you always choose people who do not see it either. When your self-esteem rises, your life will follow.

" I am self-propelled, Shield from within. I appreciate people's opinions, but I am not attached to them. I learned a long time ago that if I give them the power to feed me, I also give them the power to starve me." ~Dr. Steve Maraboli

CHAPTER SEVENTEEN

Celebrate Everything!

"Joy is what happens to us when we allow ourselves to recognize how good things really are."
~ Marianne Williamson

I want to acknowledge you for getting to the end of this book. It takes real courage to endure the discomfort of self-discovery. You continued to show up, to look and to be brave.

As you stay committed to taking actions for creating the life you love, remember to acknowledge and celebrate yourself along the way. One of the key aspects to playing big and not playing small is a willingness to acknowledge and celebrate yourself. In striving for progress, not perfection, we must see what that progress is so that we can build upon our successes.

And whenever you find yourself doubting how much further you can go, remember how far you have already come. Remember everything you have faced, all the battles you have won, and all the fears you have overcome! Nothing has broken you in the past, and it will not in the future unless you let it.

Follow the crumbs of joy and celebrate every step. Celebrate every bit of progress. Have a *Celebration Journal* that you keep with you. A good place to keep your *Celebration Journal* list is on your phone. Set reminders in your phone so you can jot down your moments throughout the day that celebrate you and your progress.

Start today! Write down three things that you want to celebrate about you and your life right now.

1. ____
   ____
2. ____
   ____
3. ____
   ____

On particularly rough days when you are sure you cannot possibly go on, remind yourself that your track record for getting through the bad days so far is one hundred percent!

As you are shifting, you will realize that you are not the same person you used to be. The things you used to tolerate have now become intolerable. Where you once remained quiet, you are now speaking your truth. Where you once battled and argued, you are now choosing to remain silent. You are beginning to understand the value of your voice, and that there are some situations that no longer deserve your time, energy and focus.

You will begin to realize what is important and what is not. You are learning to care less about what other people think of you and more about what you think of yourself. You realize how far you have come, and you remember when you thought things were such a mess that you would never recover. And you smile. You smile because you are truly proud of yourself and the person you have fought to become.

"When nobody else celebrates you, learn to celebrate yourself. When nobody else compliments you, then compliment yourself. It is not up to other people to keep you encouraged. It is up to you. Encouragement comes from the inside." ~Joel Osteen

It is amazing to me when I tackled my need to comfort eat that it was not just the challenging emotions that I would comfort myself with food or booze; it was also the extremely positive ones. I was shocked to discover that I would want to bring myself down from the feelings of extreme love, accomplishment, pride, or joy. Remember what I said about our thermostat? Without knowing it, I had decided what degree of a person I was and what degree of emotions it was okay for me to experience. As I look back and see, I think they came from fear of having depression since I was six. Depression felt like something that would take hold of me. As I was still in survival mode, it felt like a life-and-death matter to avoid any feelings linked to depression. I was terrified to experience sadness, discouragement, failure, defeat. I was sure that I was only one or two depressive episodes away from losing myself even more or completely.

So that explained my concerns about experiencing those challenging emotions. But why the heck would I not allow myself to be with and see all the good stuff?! Funny enough, it felt equally uncomfortable to feel extreme happiness or extreme sadness. Any intense emotion made me feel out of control.

If you look at your life, do you see areas that you downplay, disassociate from, or do you numb the really good stuff?______

____

____

____

Decide today that you will show up in your life one hundred percent. Decide today that you will show up *for yourself* one hundred percent. The decisions you make today shape the story of your life tomorrow. Accept where you are right now and recognize that the person you are today is evolving into the complete person you were designed to be. Trust yourself!

At the soul level, you know what is required for the journey between where you are now and where you want to be. Trust me when I say you deserve the life you were born to live and the world needs the woman that you were born to be!

"Remember when you were a child? And you lived wild and free? Your imagination carried you across galaxies. You danced before you walked, before you crawled, before you talked because your body was your language. Your expression: a moving message. Then somewhere along your journey the dreams that made your hearts soar became someone else's shadow and you forever closed the door. They said: grow up. They said: learn to be strong. Sit still, don't move, behave yourself or something's wrong. And just like that we stopped expressing. And ever since we've been searching, searching for what's missing. When we are nature by nature, greatness by design, these truths we are all born with, they were never left behind. No need to prove your worth, your heart is meant to be played. So play it out loud and let your symphony take shape. We are brilliant beyond comprehension. Just take a deep breath and you'll find your direction. My body is my vessel of expression to celebrate everything I truly am. The freedom, love and connection, waiting for me to take a stand. Now is the time to change the world as we know it. So let's dance with all our might and leave the words to the poets. What are you waiting for? All you need is within. Welcome home to your own skin. Let's begin" ~Kinrgy

Acknowledgments

A heart-felt thank you to my amazing Editor and new best friend Beverley Hotchkiss. Your talent and ability to make my words sound exactly how I meant them amazed me! You were always there when I needed extra input and helped me overcome that nasty imposter syndrome. You are a warrior for women and the world is a better place with you in it!

And to the incredible staff at Self-Publishing School, thank you for helping make dreams come true and helping me bring my book to the world! Your passion for making a difference inspires me!

Finding Self
"It's time to matter!"

ABOUT THE AUTHOR

Believing that you must first lead yourself to better lead others, Brandy Douglas Corcoran assumes a continuous commitment to studying business and life mastery with a diverse and eclectic approach towards transformation and healing. Having earned her Master's in Spiritual Psychology from the University of Santa Monica, her passion for growth and life-changing learning has led to ongoing education with Landmark Worldwide and other prominent leaders in the field of personal and professional development.

Brandy Douglas Corcoran speaks and coaches with an empathetic, non-judgmental and authentic way of being that resonates with everyone. She had walked the walk, way before she talked the talk.

From acting out as a child to a depressed, suicidal teen and then spending years as an exhausted, burnt-out wife and mother, Brandy relates to needing hope and to wanting more from life. She knows firsthand the experience of believing you are trapped by circumstance and of never feeling good enough.

FINDING SELF, her Writing, Coaching and Speaking company, established from over thirty years of experience in leadership, psychology, and personal growth, empowers people to heal and be free. Creating an experience of openness and acceptance, Brandy helps us discover new possibilities and transforms how we view ourselves, others and the world.

Brandy Douglas Corcoran inspires people to find happiness in the present while giving them the tools to create a life they love and the desire to step powerfully into their greatness!

Can You Help?

Thank You For Reading My Book!

I really appreciate all of your feedback, and I would love to hear the impact this book had on you.

Please leave me an honest review on Amazon letting me know what you thought of the book.

Thanks so much!

Brandy Douglas Corcoran

LET'S MAKE LIFE EVEN EASIER!

Reading this book is awesome but real change for *your life* happens when *you* do the work for yourself. The workbook portion within this book is designed for you to know *you* better and to create lasting breakthroughs.

I want to make that even easier with a handy workbook as my gift of thanks to you for getting my book.
Please download the Finding Self Workbook here:
brandyc.authorchannel.co

This workbook should be used alongside your book and it will help do the work to get back to *you*!
With inspirational quotes and workbook portions clearly laid out, you will have everything you need at your fingertips.

DON'T WAIT!

Say "YES" to creating a life you love:
Get started on your journey of self-discovery and find joy, fulfillment and how to love everything about your life today!
Girl, it's time to matter!

Manufactured by Amazon.ca
Bolton, ON